The Handbook for DofE Leaders

This *Handbook* provides advice and guidance for Duke of Edinburgh's Award (DofE) Leaders to set up and run a DofE group.

The Duke of Edinburgh's Award is a voluntary, non-competitive programme of activities for anyone aged 14-24. Doing their DofE gives young people the opportunity to experience new activities or develop existing skills. There are three progressive levels of programmes which when successfully completed lead to a Bronze, Silver or Gold Award. Young people create their own DofE programme by choosing a volunteering, physical and skills activity, going on an expedition and, for their Gold only, taking part in a residential activity.

The Duke of Edinburgh's Award was founded by HRH The Duke of Edinburgh in 1956 and the programme is delivered under licence by over 400 partners who offer it through DofE groups in youth clubs, voluntary organisations, schools, colleges, Young Offender Institutes and businesses.

Currently over 275,000 young people are doing their DofE in the UK, and over 65,000 achieve a Bronze, Silver or Gold Award each year. They are supported by over 50,000 Leaders.

D1368972

Our Mission
To inspire, guide and support young people in their self-development and recognise their achievements.

Foreword

Young people growing up in this modern, complicated world have many difficulties to face, and opportunities for personal achievement are often limited. At the same time, parents, teachers, voluntary organisation leaders and employers, who recognise their responsibilities towards young people, also have their challenges.

This programme is intended to help both the young as well as those who are concerned for their welfare. The object is to provide an introduction to worthwhile leisure activities and voluntary service; as a challenge to the individual to discover the satisfaction of achievement and as a guide for those people and organisations who would like to encourage the development of their younger fellow citizens.

I hope that all those who take part in this programme will find an added purpose and pleasure in their lives. I am quite sure that all those who help to run it will gain that special sense of satisfaction which comes from helping others to discover hidden abilities and to overcome a challenge.

Introduction

from Debra Searle MBE, Trustee

The Duke of Edinburgh's Award enables a young person to develop their mind, body and soul in a non-competitive environment. Its ability to elevate their self-confidence, skills and aspirations should never be underestimated, as I discovered for myself while undertaking my Gold programme. The whole experience had an amazing influence on my life and I enjoyed every section.

The Expedition section was life-changing for me and ignited a passion in me to become a professional adventurer. It is a career I have enjoyed for many years now. Without the chance to prove myself through achieving my Gold Award I doubt I would have rowed the Atlantic single-handed, sailed around Antarctica or completed the world's longest canoe race. I still use the skills today that my DofE Leader taught me all those years ago on Dartmoor.

The Volunteering section of my Gold also taught me valuable lessons about the importance of giving back to the community and this has stayed with me into adulthood. I was so delighted to read in a recent DofE survey that I am not alone and that a wonderful 61% of Award holders go on to volunteer in their local community. Just imagine what an impact it would have on our society and the economy if every young person in the UK had the opportunity to have a DofE volunteering experience. It is aspirations like this that inspire me to commit wholeheartedly to volunteering as a DofE Trustee.

I am just one of millions of people who have been privileged to have experienced DofE programmes, thanks to the generosity of volunteers and supporting organisations. None of this would be possible without you. I would like to thank and congratulate you if you are a DofE Leader or if you are considering becoming one and joining us in our work.

This *Handbook* should tell you everything you need to know about The Duke of Edinburgh's Award; its structure, the programmes, how to run and maintain a group and your role as a Leader. I have a feeling this is a book I am personally going to get to know very well as I look to become a DofE Leader myself – a role that will be very different from my role as Trustee but one that I am sure I will find just as rewarding.

Please do make the most of your time with us. Like the young people we will lead, we're about to embark on an adventure that will fill us with unique experiences, memories and a genuine sense of achievement. Thank you and best wishes in your endeavours.

Debra Searle

Contents

Chapter 1: Introducing The Duke of Edinburgh's Award

1.1 DofE programmes 2
1.2 Our guiding principles 3
1.3 The benefits 4
1.4 Our structure 5
1.5 Your Operating Authority (OA) 6

Chapter 2: Starting and leading a DofE group

2.1 What makes a DofE Leader? 10
2.2 Your role and responsibilities 10
2.3 Getting your group started 14
2.4 Parents, carers and guardians 15
2.5 Participation fees 16
2.6 Record Book Packs 16
2.7 Making participation affordable 17
2.8 Volunteers 17

Chapter 3: DofE programmes

3.1 What is a DofE programme? 22
3.2 Programme structure 23
3.3 Time and age requirements 24
3.4 When and how young people can do their DofE 28
3.5 Choosing activities 29
3.6 Setting a challenging programme 30
3.7 Activities undertaken prior to entry 30
3.8 Taking a break 31
3.9 The process for a DofE programme 31
3.10 Changing activities 33
3.11 Authorisation of Awards 33
3.12 Starting the next level 33

Chapter 4: The sections in detail

4.1   Your responsibilities as participants undertake their sections 36
4.2   The right choices for the right sections 37
4.3   Timescales and dates.. 37
4.4   Volunteering 39
4.5   Physical.. 47
4.6   Skills.. 55
4.7   Expedition 63
4.8   Residential (Gold level only).. 81

Chapter 5: Completion, recognition and progression

5.1   Helping participants to complete their DofE 90
5.2   Sectional certificates.. 94
5.3   Achieving an Award 94
5.4   Progression 95
5.5   Certificates, badges and Award presentations 95
5.6   Lost Record Books, certificates and badges 96
5.7   Life after Gold.. 96

Chapter 6: Other important information and sources of support

6.1   Empowering young people.. 100
6.2   Support from your Operating Authority 100
6.3   Support from the DofE Charity.. 102
6.4   Expedition Areas and Co-ordinators 104
6.5   Complaints, feedback and enquiries... 104
6.6   National information desk 104
6.7   The International Award Association 105
6.8   Links with other programmes 105
6.9   Approved Activity Providers 105
6.10   Commercial partners 106
6.11   DofE policies 106

Appendices

       DofE contact details 114
       Glossary of roles and terminology.. 115
       Index 116

"I chose to volunteer for the Score Project because I have a laugh whilst helping others. We get to share our skills while learning new skills and helping others in different ways. I didn't know how to approach people of different ages before and now I have the patience of teaching new skills."

Faisal, DofE participant

Chapter 1
Introducing The Duke of Edinburgh's Award

1.1   DofE programmes 2
1.2   Our guiding principles.....................................3
1.3   The benefits..4
1.4   Our structure 5
1.5   Your Operating Authority (OA)..........................6

Whilst having a passion for helping young people to achieve is essential, so too is understanding the way in which we help people and work with others.

This handbook will provide you with all the information you need to be a DofE Leader and run DofE programmes with your group. Read on and you'll discover how the DofE works, what your responsibilities are as a Leader and how we can support you in your work.

Please do take the time to familiarise yourself with its contents as it is essential that all groups offer consistently high levels of service and support. This ensures that all participants receive a high quality, enjoyable and safe DofE experience.

Thank you for volunteering; it means so much to both our participants and The Duke of Edinburgh's Award Charity. Your commitment and efforts are greatly appreciated.

DofE programmes

The concept of the DofE is simple – anyone aged between 14 and 24 can do a programme at one of three progressive levels which, when successfully completed, lead to a Bronze, Silver or Gold Duke of Edinburgh's Award.

There are four sections at Bronze and Silver level and five at Gold.

With your assistance, participants select and set objectives in each of the following areas:

Volunteering: undertaking service to individuals or the community.

Physical: improving in an area of sport, dance or fitness activities.

Skills: developing practical and social skills and personal interests.

Expedition: planning, training for and completion of an adventurous journey in the UK or abroad.

At Gold level, participants must do an additional fifth **Residential** section, which involves staying and working away from home doing a shared activity.

Each section must be done for a minimum period of time. It must be monitored and then assessed by someone with knowledge of that particular activity to achieve an Award.

Each progressive level demands more time and commitment from participants.

Our guiding principles

At the DofE we strive to achieve our mission through personal development programmes and the assessment and presentation of Awards.

All our programmes are driven by the following ten guiding principles, which are at the heart of everything we do.

1: Non-competitive

A DofE programme is a personal challenge and not a competition against others. Every participant's programme is tailor-made to reflect their individual starting point, abilities and interests.

2: Achievable by all

A Duke of Edinburgh's Award is achievable by any young person who chooses to take up its challenge, regardless of ability, gender, background or location.

3: Voluntary

Whilst DofE programmes may be offered within school, college, work time, custody or extra-curricular activity, young people choose to do a programme and commit some of their free time to undertake their activities.

4: Personal development

A DofE programme inspires personal and social development. The value to young people is dependent on personal commitment, the learning process and the quality of the experience.

5: Personalised

Young people design their own programme, which can be tailored to suit their personal circumstances, choices and local provision. They start at whichever level suits them best and they can take as long as they wish (within the age limits) to achieve an Award.

6: Balanced

Our aim is to ensure that participants experience development of the whole person; mind, body and soul. By undertaking activities focusing on at least four different aspects of development, young people complete a balanced and wide-ranging programme.

7: Progressive

At each level of engagement, a DofE programme demands progressively more time, commitment and responsibility from the participant.

8: Achievement focused

Before starting an activity, young people are encouraged to set their own challenging goals. If they aim for these goals and show improvement they will achieve a Duke of Edinburgh's Award.

9: Demand commitment

A DofE programme demands persistence and commitment and cannot be completed with a short burst of enthusiasm. Participants are encouraged to continue with activities and to maintain their interest beyond their programme requirements.

10: Enjoyable

Young people and Leaders should find participation enjoyable, fulfilling and rewarding.

The benefits

There are so many rewards for young people who do DofE programmes and achieve an Award. Its balanced programme of activities develops the whole person – mind, body and soul, in an environment of social interaction and team working.

Furthermore, as doing their DofE involves developing a personal programme of challenging activities, participants will enjoy unique experiences and rewards. However, having spoken with Award holders there is general agreement that participation develops:

- Self-belief
- Self-confidence
- A sense of identity
- Independence of thought and action
- Respect and understanding of people from different backgrounds, cultures and walks of life
- A sense of responsibility

- An awareness of their potential
- New talents and abilities
- An understanding of strengths and weaknesses
- The ability to plan and use time effectively
- The ability to learn from and give to others in the community
- New relationships
- Skills including problem solving, presentation and communication
- The ability to lead and work as part of a team.

There are plenty of benefits for you too. You'll have the satisfaction of knowing you have made a difference to someone's life. You'll see that glow and sense of pride participants have when they realise they've just done something they never imagined they could do. And of course you'll play a pivotal role in helping a young person to develop the skills and attitudes they need to succeed in life. Ask any DofE Leader and they'll tell you that gives them an unbeatable sense of achievement.

Our structure

The chart below outlines how the DofE is structured and the people and organisations you will come into contact and work with as you deliver DofE programmes. Please familiarise yourself with this as we will refer to these roles throughout this *Handbook*.

Organisation:

DofE Group
A group of ideally 15-20 young people who are working on their DofE programmes together with one DofE Leader. In a large DofE centre they may be grouped by peer groups, ages or levels. Groups may be split into teams for certain activities, i.e. volunteering or their expedition.

DofE Centre
The location where the DofE is run, for example, a school, youth centre, Young Offender Institute. There may be one or more groups at a centre dependent on the size of the centre/number of participants. This may be different for a uniformed group.

Operating Authority (OA)
The Operating Authority holds the licence to manage the delivery of DofE programmes and authorise Awards, for example, a local authority, voluntary organisation or independent school.

The DofE Charity
Head Office and 11 Regional/Country Offices deal with overall policy and central administration. A Board of Trustees governs the DofE Charity. It determines the criteria and maintains the integrity and quality of The Duke of Edinburgh's Award.

Person:

DofE Leader
The adult responsible for a DofE group. They lead, guide and encourage young people, agree their programme choices and sign off *Record Books* before giving them to their DofE Co-ordinator. They may have other adults who assist them.

DofE Co-ordinator
This person sets up and manages the DofE in a centre. They support Leaders, oversee the groups and send *Record Books* to their Operating Authority for authorisation of a full Award.

DofE Manager
The person in an OA who is responsible for the day-to-day delivery of the DofE. Your contact may be a local co-ordinator or administrator rather than the DofE Manager. There will often be other assistants and staff involved.

Chairman of Trustees, ten Trustees, Chief Executive, 100 Staff
Your Operating Authority will mainly have contact with your DofE Regional/Country Office or, in the case of national voluntary organisations, with Head Office.

Please note, these roles are not mutually exclusive. For example:
- *In a small centre there may only be one group and therefore, as a Leader, you may also assume the Co-ordinator role.*
- *An independent school that holds its own licence will be both the OA and the DofE centre. In this case, the DofE Manager and Co-ordinator is likely to be the same person, with other DofE Leaders involved with groups.*

In the UK there are over 400 Operating Authorities. DofE programmes are run in over 11,000 DofE centres from youth clubs, voluntary organisations and schools to Young Offender Institutes and businesses.

Your Operating Authority (OA)

Every centre and group must be authorised by an Operating Authority (OA) and the DofE Manager will be your main contact and source of support.

To get a licence, OAs must satisfy us that they understand the full implications of running DofE programmes.

They must:
- Be able to safeguard young people
- Maintain the DofE's aims and standards
- Have relevant policies and procedures in place
- Have an administrative framework to function correctly and ensure continuity.

As part of their licence renewal process, Operating Authorities monitor quality levels in the delivery of the DofE within their authorised centres/groups.

Evidencing a high quality experience for young people is necessary to support this process.

Further information on possible methods of monitoring and evaluating performance can be obtained from your DofE Manager.

Please see chapter six for full details of your Operating Authority's responsibilities and the support it can give you.

The Handbook for *DofE* Leaders

"It's great to see the students get enthusiastic. One of the most rewarding things is watching them struggling and overcoming it. It's good to see them put in situations that they'd never have otherwise been involved in like the expedition and volunteering – it makes them realise how lucky they are."
Julie Balchin, DofE Leader

Chapter 2

Starting and leading a DofE group

From the skills you need to be a Leader through to your ongoing responsibilities, this chapter takes you through the basics of starting and leading a DofE group.

2.1	What makes a DofE Leader?	10
2.2	Your role and responsibilities	10
2.3	Getting your group started	14
2.4	Parents, carers and guardians	15
2.5	Participation fees	16
2.6	Record Book Packs	16
2.7	Making participation affordable	17
2.8	Volunteers	17

What makes a DofE Leader?

Almost anyone with the desire to help young people develop can be a DofE Leader. We don't expect you to be able to climb mountains or survive for days in the wild. In fact you don't need any special skills or qualifications at all. If you do have a particular talent, we see that as a bonus.

The most important thing we look for is whether you really get a buzz out of helping young people improve themselves. Because, if you have that, your Operating Authority (OA) will provide the training and support you need.

Operating Authorities and the DofE have safeguarding and child protection policies and procedures that include vetting the suitability of Co-ordinators, Leaders and any other adult volunteers as part of the recruitment process. Your OA or DofE Co-ordinator will explain this and help you complete the relevant checks before you become involved.

"I love working with young people and the fact that it gives them so much. It is a wonderful programme for them and I think so much of it."
Sue Rose, DofE Leader

Your role and responsibilities

As a DofE Leader you play a crucial role in the success of your DofE group and participants' programmes. You are its focus and manager. Success will be made easier with the support of other adult volunteers. You and/ or your DofE Co-ordinator will need to recruit and train them, encourage teamwork and delegate responsibility.

You'll find a list of key DofE Leader responsibilities below. Whilst you can choose to delegate them amongst your team of volunteers, it's important that they are all done.

Safeguarding participants is paramount

The safety and welfare of your group's participants is your primary concern at all times. Operating Authorities and The Duke of Edinburgh's Award have safeguarding and child protection policies and procedures that you must adhere to.

For further information on the Code of Behaviour for DofE Leaders and volunteers see chapter six, page 108.

Given the scope and breadth of DofE programmes, participants may undertake activities that are not directly managed or organised by your group, centre or OA. In such cases, parents and guardians of those under 18 must be informed that it is their responsibility (not yours) to ensure the activity is appropriately managed and insured.

Make it enjoyable and successful

Your role is to encourage and inspire young people at every stage of their adventure. From getting their interest in the first place, to helping them choose activities which interest them and set goals, to providing the support they need to achieve, you'll play a key role in their development.

Alongside inspiring participants you'll also need to keep a close eye on their progress, assist with any issues through regular meetings and chats and help them to complete their DofE programme.

Recognise and reward achievement

The DofE is all about personal achievement, which is why it's important to recognise every single success of a participant's journey. As well as verbal encouragement, you may choose to use sectional certificates, which let them know they're a significant step closer to reaching their goals.

See chapter five for more information on sectional certificates.

And, of course, when a participant does achieve their Award, it's essential that their efforts are acknowledged. You and/or your centre may hold presentations and your OA can help you organise high-profile Award presentations to give your participants the recognition they deserve.

Keep in touch

As a DofE Leader, it's important to be aware of participants' attendance throughout their involvement with the DofE. If someone isn't attending as regularly as they normally would, get in touch to find out why. They might just need a gentle nudge to get back on track. It's important to think about how they might respond best – a text or email may be far more effective than a phone call or letter!

If a participant moves to a new area, help them make contact with a local DofE centre via an OA so they can complete their programme and achieve their Award.

*Our website contains contact information for all OAs throughout the UK – **www.DofE.org/contact***

Encourage completion

When young people sign up to do their DofE they do so with an expectation that they will complete it. Whilst we accept that a small number of participants will not see their programme through to the end, it is essential that as many as possible achieve their Award. It is your responsibility as their DofE Leader to help them achieve this.

See chapter five for hints and tips on how to achieve higher completion rates.

Encourage progression

When a participant has completed one level of programme and achieved an Award, it's important that you remind them about the next level and actively encourage them to get started on it.

Maintain standards and keep in touch with developments

As a DofE Leader, you'll enjoy a high degree of autonomy but it's crucial that whatever you do meets our national standards. So please make sure that everything your group does is in accordance with the DofE's, your OA's and your centre's requirements, policies and procedures. It's vital that you fully understand all insurance issues too. Your DofE Co-ordinator and/or OA can help you with this.

Through regular contact, newsletters etc. your centre Co-ordinator and OA's DofE Manager will keep you informed of all relevant matters. You can also find key information on our website and by signing up for your free copy of our magazine for DofE Leaders and regular e-newsletter at **www.DofE.org/leaders**

Keep a firm handle on your group's resources and activities

Maintaining a tight grip on your group's finances is vital for delivering services efficiently. Please stick to your OA's and/or centre's policies and procedures in these matters.

The processing and maintenance of procedures, records and details is vital too. Keep copies of your group's enrolment forms, parental consent forms and activity sheets.

All *Record Books* must be kept up to date, forwarded to your DofE Co-ordinator/OA and returned promptly to your participants in order to help them progress through their programmes and achieve their Awards.

Stay in touch with your community

Keep an eye out for activities that your group and participants could become involved with around your community. This will be made easier by promoting The Duke of Edinburgh's Award locally and publicising any newsworthy activities and participant achievements. By raising your profile it's likely that organisations and individuals will start contacting you with offers of help.

Actively seeking sponsors and partners could help your group/centre in its work. This could take the form of equipment donations, event sponsorship, use of facilities, providing additional activities, general support and volunteering opportunities. Again, raising your group's profile can help you in this area.

See chapter six for more ideas on how to get your activities noticed.

Maintain and improve services

We are committed to constantly maintaining and improving our services. To monitor and improve the quality of DofE programmes please find out what your participants think of their own programmes. Encourage them to express their opinions through comments in their *Record Books*, peer reviews, one-to-one sessions, group discussions, self-evaluations, and other appropriate methods.

Getting your group started

There are different ways to set up your DofE group and each one has unique considerations. Depending on your situation you'll need to do things slightly differently:

- In an existing DofE centre, where there is a need for another group to meet demand from participants. *Your DofE centre will already be authorised to run the DofE – please talk to your DofE Co-ordinator who will explain how the DofE works, who your OA is, help you set up your group and ensure that all checks are undertaken.*
- A centre where young people already meet, when you want to introduce the DofE to them. *If this is the case, please contact your local Operating Authority for authorisation to set up a DofE centre and group(s).*
- You want to set up the DofE in your area and are not based at an existing place where young people meet. *You'll need to contact your local Operating Authority for authorisation to set up a DofE centre and group(s) and find a venue.*

If you have any issues or concerns or are unsure who your Operating Authority is, please contact your DofE Regional/Country Office – *contact details can be found on page 114.*

Contact details for Operating Authorities can be found at
www.DofE.org/contact

"You don't need a great deal of specialist resources to get started and once you're in the network, you'll probably find that other DofE groups are happy to share. It's important that you have enough adult support to ensure safety and encourage variety. It's also useful to think ahead – DofE has a habit of growing!"
Lister Baynes, DofE volunteer

Getting the right location is crucial

Your group must be based somewhere easily accessible for all participants, e.g. a school, youth centre, commercial premises or sports centre. Wherever possible, it should be somewhere that young people would like to meet. It must also be in a safe environment – both the meeting place, as well as its immediate surroundings.

Getting participants involved

Unless you have a ready-made group you're taking over or lots of young people just waiting for someone to lead them, you'll need to get young people interested. You can do this in many ways, depending on your situation. For example, you can organise taster evenings, events and presentations, put up posters, announce it over the school loudspeaker system or on your youth group's blog.

Existing Award holders are often happy to give first-hand accounts of their experiences – it's a very successful way of attracting new young people. It's also well worth encouraging local businesses to talk about how achieving an Award can benefit a young person's CV. You can also use the local press, radio and the internet to promote your DofE group.

See chapter six for more ideas on generating publicity.

Don't forget – the DofE is open to any young person aged 14-24, regardless of background, location or ability.

Please read our full Equal Opportunities policy in chapter six.

As it opens the door to unique experiences, achieving an Award often brings children and their parents, carers and guardians closer together. So be sure to encourage involvement in their children's activities – be it by simply voicing their approval, driving them around or encouraging them to keep going.

Parents, carers and guardians can also be a great help to your DofE group/ centre. From assisting with admin or driving minibuses to training or fundraising, there's so much they could do. As their children are involved it's quite likely that they'd be interested in lending a hand, so encourage them to volunteer in any way they can.

Parents, carers and guardians

Parental Consent

You'll need parental consent if participants under 18 want to join your group. As the DofE Leader, you must ensure that parents, carers and guardians are always kept fully informed regarding their child's DofE activities.

How parents, carers and guardians can make a difference

The support of parents, carers and guardians can make a big difference to a young person's experience of the programme. It's important that they encourage their children and acknowledge their achievements at every stage.

> *"The DofE really is for anyone. My daughter has made so many new friends and discovered loads of new talents she might not otherwise have realised she had."*
> Dave Ludlow, parent

Participation fees

To take part in the DofE, participants pay a nominal fee. This fee is their contribution towards the Charity's costs in running their DofE programme and represents a personal commitment adding value to their involvement. The fee represents a very small proportion of the overall cost which is supported by the funds raised by the DofE Charity. The current charge for participation can be found at *www.DofE.org*

Your OA and/or centre may add a small administration fee to this amount and they must explain this clearly to participants. You can choose to do the same or charge a weekly subscription fee to cover any extra costs. If this is the case, you must tell the young person and their parent/carer/guardian how much has been added and what it is for.

As the DofE Leader, it is your responsibility to collect and pass each participant's fee to your DofE Co-ordinator/OA. In some centres, the Co-ordinator may handle this for all groups. Once your OA has received it, they will send your participant's *Record Book Pack*, making them officially DofE participants.

Record Book Packs

A participant's *Record Book*, contained in the *Record Book Pack*, is their log book for their DofE programme. The pack also contains background information about the DofE, activity ideas for each section and advice on planning and recording progress and achievement.

All a participant's activities, experiences, comments and personal achievements should be noted in the *Record Book*. Details should include the start and finish dates for each section, details of any training courses undertaken or qualifications they've gained. A participant's *Record Book* will need signatures from you and/or their Assessors *(see page 18 for details on Assessors)* whenever they complete a section of their programme. Additional remarks or comments should be positive and encouraging. When they have completed all sections for their current level, your OA will use it to authorise the young person's Duke of Edinburgh's Award.

If at first a participant doesn't achieve a particular section, the Assessor should discuss the reasons with them and only make an entry in the *Record Book* once they have successfully completed it.

Making participation affordable

It is usually programme activities, rather than the cost of enrolment, that can make the greatest financial demands on participants. Encouraging them to devise a programme that matches their resources is all part of the challenge. However, more costly activities can be attainable and many participants organise fundraising events for special activities.

Some grant giving bodies will provide funds and many companies sponsor young people's activities. Additionally, participants may have access to certain equipment through your centre or OA. So if they do have ambitious plans there's still every chance of realising them, they'll just need to be resourceful!

Volunteers

Building your team of volunteers and helpers

Groups do what they do thanks to their team of volunteers. As a DofE Leader you'll have to motivate and organise them. You may also be in charge of recruitment and training of the team. It's important that you take a hands-on role in this area. Always look for individuals who share your interest in helping young people. It's important that they are appropriate to work with young people, have a passion for our work and know how to connect with current and potential participants.

Get to know a volunteer's individual skills. Then you'll be more able to give them roles that best fit their talents and the needs of your group. From minibus drivers and admin support to activity leaders and Assessors, there are countless ways for people to get involved. It's definitely a case of the more the merrier.

Don't forget the people who can't commit to turning up every week. They could help in many other ways. For example, there's fundraising for your group's/centre's activities, making the teas on an open day or running a presentation skills training session for your group before their expedition. Just think creatively!

Above and beyond recruitment and management of volunteers, you'll also build relationships with key supporters – from senior staff in your centre to funders and your community. Keep them up-to-date with the developments and requirements of your group.

More specialist support

As a DofE Leader you can't be there every minute of every day for every participant throughout the entirety of their programme. That's why when participants select an activity they need to ensure that they have a suitable Assessor in place, plus potentially a Supervisor as well.

These are not mutually exclusive roles. One person can do one or all of them. And, in certain situations and sections, you may find that you are best placed to take on all of these roles.

Before working with your group, anyone involved in supervising and assessing participants must be checked and approved by your OA as suitably experienced or qualified. Remember, if the participant is arranging their own activity, then their parents/carers/guardians are responsible for safeguarding but you as their Leader or your centre's Co-ordinator should check the Assessor's experience/qualifications.

Furthermore, prior to helping your participants it's crucial that volunteers are fully briefed regarding their roles and responsibilities. Make sure they understand the details of participants' programmes.

You may need to organise extra training to bring volunteers up to speed.

Our guides to each section for Leaders and volunteers (see **www.DofE.org/shop**) are also really useful for someone who's only going to be helping with just one section.

"Helping out with DofE participants is such a rewarding thing to do. It's great to watch their progression and see their confidence grow. Often, when they start out, they know nothing of the skill and aren't confident in their abilities but when they complete their finished pieces you can see the sense of pride in what they've achieved."
Rob Young, DofE Assessor

Assessors

An Assessor checks on a young person's progress and agrees the completion of a section of their programme. They will sign the participant's *Record Book* to confirm this.

An Assessor can be anyone who is interested in helping a young person to achieve, has some knowledge of the activity they are doing and can be available over the time they're doing it. From the local football club manager to a charity shop manager, from the

The Handbook for *DofE* Leaders

neighbour who's a web designer to the conservation expert leading a residential week, just about anyone can be an Assessor for the Volunteering, Physical, Skills and Residential sections. However, to maintain the integrity and value of Duke of Edinburgh's Awards, they must be independent. Therefore, they cannot be a family member of a participant.

Because of the nature of expeditions, there are slightly different rules in place for Expedition Assessors – *please see page 76 for full information.*

If you are struggling to find Assessors, talk to your centre's DofE Co-ordinator and/or OA's DofE Manager – many of whom will have contacts and lists of people that have been an Assessor before.

The Assessor should have knowledge of the activity being undertaken and be aware of the young person's objectives. They should also be available at key stages throughout the experience in order to assess the participant's contribution and development. Once a section is complete the Assessor will meet with the young person to discuss their performance, their experiences and achievements.

The Assessor will also decide whether the participant has met the DofE requirements – that they've demonstrated effort, perseverance, improvement and made progress towards their section goals. This information, along with comments from the Assessor and participant, is written in their *Record Book*, and signed by both of them.

If you are not the Assessor, then as their DofE Leader you must organise a meeting with the participant to discuss their experiences on completion of each section.

Note: Expedition Assessors must also be accredited through The Duke of Edinburgh's Award Assessor Accreditation Scheme.
*See **www.DofE.org/training***

Supervisors

These are people with a good understanding of a participant's chosen activities. A Supervisor is essential for the Expedition section as they are responsible for supervising and supporting a team of participants to ensure their safety and well-being whilst they are doing their expedition.

In the case of the Volunteering or Residential sections a Supervisor will most likely be connected with the organisation/activity the participant intends to work with. They will help set goals and regularly meet with the young person to check on their progress, address any potential issues and adjust goals.

Please see pages 75 and 76 for the more detailed roles Supervisors and Assessors have for the Expedition section.

So now you have a venue, lots of participants eager to start, volunteers keen to help you and the go-ahead from your OA. Over the next two chapters we'll cover DofE programmes in detail, so you're ready to give your participants all the support and encouragement they need.

"My favourite activity has been hockey for my Physical. I've been playing since I was ten and have loved it for many years. I really enjoy working so hard and then achieving and I love the team aspect of it – all working together for the same goals makes for a great atmosphere."

Rebecca, DofE participant

Chapter 3
DofE programmes

So what is a DofE programme? How old do participants need to be before they start? What do they need to bear in mind when choosing activities? This chapter will tell you all about the programmes, what they involve and how the process works.

3.1   What is a DofE programme?............................22
3.2   Programme structure......................................23
3.3   Time and age requirements 24
3.4   When & how young people can do their DofE ...28
3.5   Choosing activities...29
3.6   Setting a challenging programme 30
3.7   Activities undertaken prior to entry.................30
3.8   Taking a break 31
3.9   The process for a DofE programme................31
3.10 Changing activities 33
3.11 Authorisation of Awards..................................33
3.12 Starting the next level 33

What is a DofE programme?

A DofE programme is the series of activities covering different categories that participants select and undertake to achieve a Bronze, Silver or Gold Duke of Edinburgh's Award. The programme is all about self-development. It's not about being first. It's non-competitive and focuses on helping young people to improve existing skills or gain new talents, abilities or perspectives and being the best they can.

Individual programmes for individual people

Developing initiative is a key part of a participant's involvement. At the start, participants take responsibility for the selection of their own programme. They should consider costs, venue choices, travel requirements and the availability of a suitable Assessor and/ or Supervisor. Whilst it is important that participants use their own initiative you will still need to provide support and advice, especially when they're devising their programme and setting objectives.

Someone with learning difficulties or limited mobility may take longer to complete a section or require extra training or support. This is not an issue – programmes are designed to be flexible. Remember, this is about young people pushing their own limits.

Though the programmes are an individual challenge there are times when participants will be required to work as a team. In these situations you should provide guidance and ensure that everyone is involved at a level that is appropriate for their development.

With regard to the programmes, the conditions detailed in this *Handbook* must be met, although it is possible to agree variations because of a young person's abilities or location.

At all levels any proposed variations should be discussed with and approved by your centre and OA. At Gold level the appropriate DofE Regional/ Country Office must be involved in the consultative process to ensure that participants receive effective guidance based on examples of good practice.

> *"'The DofE is about trying to help young people help themselves to become well balanced, healthy individuals that have a sense of social and environmental responsibility."*
> John Hender, DofE Leader

Programme structure

Levels

There are three separate, progressive levels of programmes, which lead to a Bronze, Silver or Gold Duke of Edinburgh's Award. The main differences between them are the minimum length of time required to complete them, the degree of challenge and the minimum age at which young people can start to do them.

"I'm so glad I did my Bronze and Silver before I tried Gold! It gave me a gentle build-up for 'the big one' – especially with the expedition. Much better than 'going in at the deep end'!"
Emma, DofE participant

Bronze, Silver and Gold levels have been created to encourage young people to develop their abilities and progress towards achievement of a Gold Award at a pace roughly commensurate with their age. The required time commitments and progress to be made at each level increases through Bronze, Silver to Gold.

Consideration should be given to abilities of young people as well as their age when introducing them to the DofE. For example, some 17/18 year olds may find it a challenge to achieve a Bronze Award in six months. As their DofE Leader, you need to bear in mind that each level can be a personal challenge for an individual, whatever their age.

Sections

Why do DofE programmes have sections? Each section focuses on developing a core aspect of a young person in a fun yet challenging manner. They have very specific aims and purposes. By doing them all, young people will help their community, develop new skills, confidence, talents and gain a greater appreciation of the world. Achieving an Award really does enrich the mind, body and soul. What's more, every step is an exciting and unique adventure.

> ### Each DofE level has four sections:
>
> ■ **Volunteering**: undertaking service to individuals or the community.
>
> ■ **Physical**: improving in an area of sport, dance or fitness activities.
>
> ■ **Skills**: developing practical and social skills and personal interests.
>
> ■ **Expedition**: planning, training for and completion of an adventurous journey in the UK or abroad.
>
> ■ At Gold level, participants must do an additional fifth **Residential** section, which involves staying and working away from home doing a shared activity.

Time and age requirements

Overall requirements

There is no real time limit when it comes to completing a DofE programme. As long as participants are under 25 years old when they complete all their activities in their programme, they are free to work at a pace that they're comfortable with and can achieve their Award.

Our only stipulation is that participants spend the following minimum time doing their programmes.

Please note that, whilst timescales are expressed in months, participants need to give a regular commitment averaging at least an hour a week during this time.

This is because to achieve an Award young people must show persistence, commitment and personal development over a period of time. It's not something that can be achieved through a short burst of enthusiasm one weekend!

	Minimum period of participation by:	
Level:	Direct entrants	Previous Award holders
Bronze	6 months	n/a
Silver	12 months	6 months
Gold	18 months	12 months
Direct entrants are young people starting their DofE programme at either Silver or Gold level, who have not achieved the previous level of Award.		

Bronze Award (14+ years old)

Three parts of the programme, Volunteering, Physical and Skills, each require a minimum of three months to complete, whilst the Expedition involves planning, training for and undertaking a two-day (one night) expedition. Participants must also decide whether to spend a further three months on the Volunteering, Physical or Skills section. The decision is entirely theirs. It must be made at the start but can be reviewed later.

It is possible to allow a young person to start their Bronze programme shortly before their 14th birthday, if they are part of a larger group that is aged 14 plus. This often happens when friends or a school year group decide to embark on their adventures together.

However, for this to be allowed, you must be sure that the young person is sufficiently mature to do their programme and also gain approval from your DofE Co-ordinator and Operating Authority.

To achieve their Award, participants must have completed their programme and be at least 14½ years old.

Volunteering	Physical	Skills	Expedition
3 months	3 months	3 months	Plan, train for and complete a 2 day, 1 night expedition
*All participants must undertake a **further** 3 months in the Volunteering, Physical or Skills section.*			

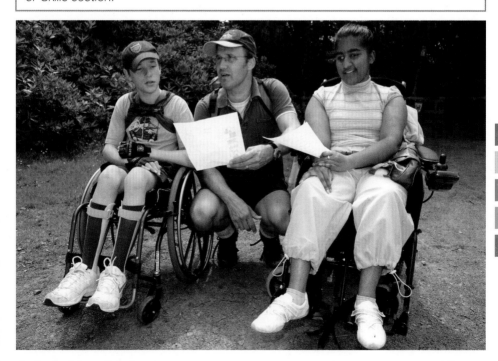

Silver Award (15+ years old)

Participants spend a minimum of six months volunteering. For the Physical and Skills sections, they must spend a minimum of six months on one and three on the other. The Expedition involves planning, training for and undertaking a three day (two night) expedition.

The decision on which section to do for the longest time is totally theirs. If they have jumped straight into their Silver programme they'll need to do a further six months either volunteering or doing whichever of the physical or skills activity they spent more time on. This decision must be made at the start but can be reviewed later.

To achieve their Award, participants must have completed their programme successfully and be at least 15½ years old if they already have Bronze. Direct entrants must be at least 16 years old before they complete their Silver programme.

OAs sometimes let young people who have achieved their Bronze Award make a start on their Silver Award before their 15th birthday. However, in such situations you must consult with your centre and OA before agreeing anything.

Volunteering	Physical	Skills	Expedition
6 months	One section for 6 months and the other section for 3 months		Plan, train for and complete a 3 day, 2 night expedition

*Direct entrants must undertake a **further** 6 months in the Volunteering or the **longer** of the Physical or Skills sections.*

The Handbook for DofE Leaders

Gold Award (16+ years old)

Participants must be at least 16 years of age to start their DofE programme at Gold level. No activities can count until their 16th birthday.

Participants spend a minimum of 12 months volunteering. For their Physical and Skills sections they must spend a minimum of 12 months on one and six on the other. Again, they decide which section to do for the longer time. They'll plan, train for and complete a four day (three night) expedition. The biggest difference at Gold is that participants must do an additional, fifth section – Residential. This is an activity away from home for five days and four nights with people they do not already know.

Direct entrants must spend a further six months either volunteering or doing whichever of the skills or physical activities they spent the most time on. This decision must be made at the start but can be reviewed later.

To achieve their Award, participants must have completed their programme successfully and be at least 17 years old if they already have their Silver Award. Direct entrants must be at least 17½ when they complete their programme.

You should encourage your participants to continue activities beyond the minimum time requirements of their programme in order to meet their personal ambitions.

Volunteering	Physical	Skills	Expedition	Residential
12 months	One section for 12 months and the other section for 6 months		Plan, train for and complete a 4 day, 3 night expedition	Undertake a shared activity in a residential setting away from home for 5 days and 4 nights

*Direct entrants must undertake a **further** 6 months in either the Volunteering or the **longer** of the Physical or Skills sections.*

Maximum Age

The upper age limit for the completion of all programmes is a young person's 25th birthday. Extensions to the upper age limit can only be considered when illness, accident or unavoidable circumstances make it impossible to complete a programme by the age of 25. In such situations, your OA must send a written request to your DofE Regional/Country Office. If the application is successful, extra time will be allowed. This must not be exceeded.

When and how young people can do their DofE

A DofE programme is all about personal choice and responsibility. Participants do their activities either in their own personal time, partly as one of a range of options in supported/core time or as an after-school programme.

Activities may even take place during school hours or working hours but participants must be able to prove that their activities still required a substantial contribution of personal time and voluntary effort.

The amount of personal time required may need to be reduced when necessary, for example, for young people with learning difficulties or where access to the facilities for an activity is constrained (e.g. by availability times or access).

They should not do activities that are entirely curriculum subjects with no extra personal effort. For example, essay writing purely based on A-level assignments is not acceptable but a programme that includes entering a school writing competition could meet the requirements.

Using programme activities as a framework to support or create an alternative curriculum or education programme, e.g. for young people at risk of exclusion, is also allowed, even if it is done in a school environment and entirely in scheduled lesson time.

Choosing activities

There is a massive choice of activities that count towards DofE programmes. Participants can select practically any activity they wish – as long as it's legal and morally acceptable. It could be something that they're currently into or a completely new area.

However, this much choice can be overwhelming, so you need to help participants select activities that they'll really enjoy and set achievable but challenging objectives.

Achieving an Award, be it Bronze, Silver or Gold, is all about personal development and that requires taking responsibility and initiative. From the start, participants must take ownership of their programmes by choosing the activities they wish to pursue in each section.

Activities are placed in specific sections for a reason. When participants are making their choices it's essential that you're on hand to advise them and support them in their decisions. This is to ensure that any choices meet section aims and requirements as well as the guiding principles of any DofE programme *(see page three).* For example, they cannot choose to do an activity for their Skills section if it is listed as a Physical section activity. You'll also need to make sure that their choice is available locally (Expedition and Residential sections aside).

Don't panic, we're not expecting you to be an expert in every section! *Chapter four will give you more guidance in this area.* You do, however, need to be

> *"Doing your DofE teaches you that ANYTHING is possible. Even if you think you can't do something, if you put your mind to it you will pull through and you will feel FANTASTIC afterwards!"*
> Wayne, Gold Award holder

aware of the aims and requirements for each section so you can advise your participants and recruit Assessors and Supervisors for any activity.

As a DofE Leader it's important that you ensure all participants get the most out of their programmes. The best way of doing this is by helping them choose a balanced range of activities.

Encourage participants to spread their wings with their choices – they shouldn't just focus on one area of interest across all the sections. For instance it's great if a participant is playing football and wishes to do this in their Physical section. However, selecting activities for every section except their expedition that focus on football is not a good move for most young people. After all, the aim is to broaden horizons and try new experiences.

Ultimately participants need to choose activities that they are going to enjoy. It could be something that they are already doing or perhaps one they've always wanted to try. There is such a wide choice that whatever they would like to do, the odds are they can.

Setting a challenging programme

When advising on a programme and objectives always bear in mind what level of expertise the young person already has, their maturity and level of confidence. The goals they set need to be challenging but achievable. If it is too unrealistic, it may in fact damage a young person's confidence and self-belief. Remember, our aim is to help young people develop themselves. This will only occur if they set realistic challenges.

If you're unsure about a certain activity – whether it's OK to do or simply which section it belongs in – contact your OA who will advise you.

The key when choosing activities is to ignite a participant's imagination. Get them really thinking about things they'd love to try or do. But equally keep their feet firmly planted in the real world. Make sure participants take into consideration their personal circumstances, local availability and potential costs when choosing.

Don't forget that OAs have overall responsibility for monitoring the quality of participants' experiences and safety. They will have additional guidelines relating to particular activities, which you will need to be familiar with and ensure are met.

*Chapter four contains more information about the detailed requirements for each section and examples of programmes for each section. More inspiring ideas can also be found at **www.DofE.org***

Once a participant has decided upon their programme, you need to review it before they start, while they're doing it and once they've finished. This is to check they are happy with their progress, the activities selected and that their objectives are challenging enough.

If required, these can always be reset to make them more challenging or achievable.

Activities undertaken prior to entry

One activity done before a young person starts their DofE programme could count towards the achievement of an Award if it was done during the preceding three months, or six months if done with an Approved Activity Provider *(see chapter six)*.

All activities must have been done in accordance with DofE programme principles, conditions and age requirements.

Taking a break

Although they should ideally progress from Bronze to Silver and then Gold, it's totally up to a participant as to when and what order they do each section within each level. As long as they complete their programme and achieve their Award before their 25th birthday, they are free to take a break for holidays, exams or if they just feel they need a rest.

The process for a DofE programme

Like most things in life, young people get out of a DofE programme what they put in. So to ensure participants get the maximum benefit out of their activities and achieve their Awards, we've devised the process below. Please follow it faithfully.

The process has four key stages that apply to all sections and activities:

1) Preparation
2) Training
3) Activity
4) Assessment

Preparation

Participants need to think about and research what they would like to do for each section. They may talk to friends and family about their ideas. It's quite likely your participants will want to talk to you too. Your role during this stage is to support and, if necessary, advise them on their choices.

Once the participant has made their decisions, arrange a meeting with them.

Alternatively ask one of your group's volunteers to do this and report back to you. During the meeting discuss the participant's choices and the commitments required. Establish that they have thoroughly researched their selection, are happy with their decisions and cover the following areas:

- **Aim:** what do they want to do/achieve? Discuss the aim and benefits of the section and how that is reflected in the young person's own programme choice.
- **Activity:** do the activities fit their personal objectives and the requirements of the DofE?
- **Details:** think about/suggest final objectives as well as interim goals and milestones. Establish, agree and write down personal goals that are practical, measurable, achievable, exciting and have realistic timings.
- **First steps:** is any training required? What about any safety or legal requirements?
- **Recording their journey:** establish a system for how the young person will record their efforts and when you will conduct regular progress reviews.
- Remind them **how their Award is authorised** and the type of celebration they can expect when they finally achieve it *(see chapter five).*

With these items discussed and agreed, your participant can design an individual programme that takes into account their needs along with the principles and requirements of a DofE programme.

Programme planners to help participants create their programme are available from **www.DofE.org/sections** – there is one for each section.

Training

There will regularly be times when a participant's choice of activity requires them to take a course, simple introduction or structured training before starting their activity. This should be understood and agreed by both the young person and you. Participants should be fully aware of the time, resources and equipment that may be required to undertake their training.

In the Volunteering section, training can count towards the time requirements as long as it is in proportion and the aim of the section is clearly achieved. Volunteering must be based around practical help to the community not just training in a skill that may help the community in the future.

See the sectional information in chapter four for more clarification.

In the Physical and Skills sections the activity may be training to achieve their goal, for example, to gain a qualification such as a music grade or sports award.

Activity

This is often the most important and enjoyable part of any section – the actual doing bit! As a DofE Leader you need to be constantly supporting and encouraging your participants.

Meet with them regularly to talk about how they're getting on, encourage and help them to sort out any problems they may be facing. These discussions will enable you to adjust programmes or goals and address any additional training or general needs that could assist their progress.

Assessment

To complete a DofE programme every activity undertaken must be successfully completed and assessed. So when the time comes to review your participant's efforts their Assessor (which may be you), you as their Leader or one of your volunteers must meet them to discuss:

- The goals that were set and what the participant actually achieved.
- What challenges were faced and how they were overcome.
- The overall experience and what they enjoyed.

The meeting also provides the perfect opportunity to celebrate the young person's achievements. It is also the ideal time to encourage them to complete their other sections, achieve their Award and progress to the next level. Remember to ensure that the Assessor, you and your participant have completed their *Record Book*. You must all add comments and sign it. Once this is done for all sections, it must be sent to your OA for authorisation.

These key stages are covered in more detail in chapter four, including the differences between each section.

Changing activities

If absolutely necessary, activities may be changed once in each section at each level. However, we would not encourage this as participants will not gain the full benefit of developing their skills and knowledge of their activities.

If a participant does need to change then they must restart the preparation, training, activity and assessment process. The timescale for the second activity will be shorter, as the two activities together will need to add up to the minimum overall time requirements for that section/level. When this occurs both activities must be recorded in their *Record Book*.

Starting the next level

Participants should be encouraged to complete their entire programme to achieve their Award before embarking on the next level. However, they may start on a section of the next level prior to completing the previous one if they:

- Have reached the minimum age of entry for the next level.
- Obtain a *Record Book* for this level
- Have completed that section of the previous Award.
- Are not working on all three levels at the same time.

Please refer to chapter five for more information on completion, recognition and progression.

Authorisation of Awards

A participant has achieved a Bronze or Silver Award when the Operating Authority confirms that all relevant conditions have been met, based on the information recorded in the *Record Book*. Each Operating Authority has its own system to manage this process, so please check with your Operating Authority.

At Gold, a Gold Award notification form (available at **www.DofE.org/gold**) must be completed and signed by the participant and you as their DofE Leader. This must then be given to your centre's Co-ordinator, who will send it to your Operating Authority with their *Record Book*.

They will then check and forward it to the appropriate DofE Regional/Country Office for final confirmation.

"Doing my DofE gave me a chance
to try out things I'd never have
thought of doing before."
Harpreet, DofE participant

Chapter 4

The sections in detail

This chapter will take you through the sections of a DofE programme in greater detail. From selecting activities, to training, doing and successful completion, this chapter gives you the information you need to deliver a fulfilling and exciting experience for all your participants.

4.1   Your responsibilities as participants
      undertake their sections...................................36
4.2   The right choices for the right sections 37
4.3   Timescales and dates....................................37
4.4   Volunteering 39
4.5   Physical...47
4.6   Skills..55
4.7   Expedition 63
4.8   Residential (Gold level only)...........................81

Your responsibilities as participants undertake their sections

As a DofE Leader, you will be expected to:

- Inspire young people to achieve their full potential.

- Help young people choose activities based on their interests, the needs of the community and personal circumstances.

- Motivate them to either create their own or take part in existing activities.

- Help them to stay safe.

- Inspire young people to complete their programme and gain a Duke of Edinburgh's Award.

- Give them the knowledge, understanding or training needed to participate and get the most from their DofE programme.

- Help them find a suitable Assessor and/or Supervisor as required to help them during their activities. The person(s) selected must have a full understanding of the activity the participant is pursuing and a desire to help young people achieve.

- Help them set appropriate and challenging personal goals for each activity.

- Make sure they put any training into practice.

- Encourage full commitment throughout their DofE programme.

- Encourage them to move on to the next level.

The right choices for the right sections

As a DofE Leader it is important that you ensure participants select the right activities for the right sections. This can be confusing and the differences may seem marginal, but making the wrong selection will ultimately mean that a young person cannot complete their programme and achieve their Award.

For instance, learning first aid is a skill but spending time as a first aider is a volunteering activity as it involves helping others. Equally, dance is a physical activity but dance appreciation would be classed as a skills activity because it is about learning theory rather than physical performance.

As their Leader, you are responsible for checking that young people's choices count towards the correct sections. All activities must fit into one of the sections. Guidance notes are available on our website **www.DofE.org/sections**

If at any time you are unsure about an activity, please consult your OA.

Timescales and dates

The minimum time requirements for every section at each level can be found in chapter three.

The start date for each section should be the date of your first preparation meeting, and the finish date is when the activity has been completed, assessed and the *Record Book* is completed.

Volunteering

Volunteering

Aim

To inspire young people to make a difference within their communities or to an individual's life and develop compassion by giving service to others. From DJing at the local hospital to assisting at an animal shelter, from renovating a heritage site to coaching sports at a youth club – the options are almost limitless.

Principles

- People have a responsibility to each other. By volunteering, communities are improved and strengthened.
- Young people are passionate about many things and should be encouraged to make a positive contribution to something they care about.
- The commitment to volunteering should be recognised; therefore young people are rewarded for this activity with the completion of a section of their DofE programme.

Benefits

Through volunteering, participants:
- Learn about their community and feel a sense of belonging and purpose.
- Learn to take responsibility for their communities and their own actions by committing and persevering with an activity.
- Build new relationships with members of their community, decreasing fears and prejudice and increasing community cohesion.
- Further understand their own strengths and weaknesses by evaluating their own progress and building confidence and self-esteem.
- Get a chance to develop teamwork and leadership skills, increasing their employability and work experience.
- Have the opportunity to trust others and in turn be trusted.
- Enjoy new adventures.

What is required?

Volunteering is simple. It's about choosing to give time to do something useful, without getting paid. It can be helping people, the community or society, the environment or animals.

Team volunteering

We know the benefits of doing an activity in a team are significant for young people. Therefore, why not encourage young people to identify a local need, plan how to meet it and then do their volunteering together?

Team volunteering may also be ideal for young people who cannot find an appropriate individual opportunity, especially if they are under 16.

An example of this could be a youth group that is concerned that their local playground is covered in graffiti and litter. Together they develop an action plan. Doing it will see them dealing with their local council and police as well as talking to local businesses about sponsoring the play equipment and bins. They can then clean up the playground with the appropriate tools and celebrate the changes and their achievements in the local paper.

More support can be found online at
www.DofE.org/leaders

This flowchart gives a simple overview of the steps involved for a young person to complete their Volunteering section. Each step is explained in more detail on the following pages.

Preparation
Young people plan their volunteering experience and set their objectives. This includes who/what they will help, what they will do, where they will do it and how long for.

↓

Training
Participants undergo any training necessary to allow them to undertake their practical volunteering activities.

↓

Activity
Participants do their practical volunteering activity regularly, averaging at least an hour a week, for the planned time.

↓

Assessment
The young person meets with their Assessor to discuss and record their experiences, how they developed and reached their goals. Their *Record Book* is completed.

The four steps to completing the Volunteering section

1. Preparation is everything

Before starting their volunteering activity participants must thoroughly research the charity, organisation or people they are helping and have an Assessor willing to support them. Their Assessor will usually be an adult in the organisation with whom the young person is volunteering, often their named contact. For team volunteering this is likely to be you.

A participant's research and understanding of who they're helping will enable them to develop goals that are achievable yet challenging. As DofE Leader you, or a nominated volunteer, should make sure that they set them with their activity Assessor and that their achievements will lead to some form of personal development. Ensure a participant's activity is focussed on skills and experience, as well as meeting the needs of others or the environment. Their volunteering activity could be individual, team or DofE group based.

2. Training may be required

The young person may require some training before starting their activity and some organisations have training courses that must be done before volunteering can start. If possible, any training undertaken should result in accreditation or a qualification. Furthermore, it should take place towards the beginning of the time period and take up no more than a quarter of the overall time.

Timescales: Volunteering

Level	Minimum time	Notes
Bronze	3 or 6 months	*Young people must do one of their Volunteering, Physical or Skills sections for 6 months, the others for 3.*
Silver	6 or 12 months	*Young people who haven't achieved Bronze must extend their Volunteering or the longer of their Physical or Skills sections to 12 months.*
Gold	12 or 18 months	*Young people who haven't achieved Silver must extend their Volunteering or the longer of their Physical or Skills sections to 18 months.*

Remember, young people must commit to regular activities averaging at least an hour a week during this time.

For example, a first aid course lasting three months would not be a suitable volunteering activity for a Bronze Award (this would be a skill). However, it is in proportion and acceptable for a Gold participant who then volunteers for St. John Ambulance for another nine months.

Volunteering must be based around practical help to the community not just training in a skill that may benefit the community in the future.

Remember, many training courses that don't count for the Volunteering section may well be acceptable as a Skills section activity if a participant wants to do it.

3. Activity – time to start volunteering!

With the research done, goals set and any required training successfully completed, your participant is ready to begin their volunteering activity. They will need to commit their personal time to doing unpaid work which benefits the environment, a community, organisation or individual.

Volunteering must not be done for a business. For example, helping at the local vets would not count, whereas time spent at an animal shelter would.

The bulk of their time should be spent actually doing the work required, such as digging out the canal, leading

The Handbook for DofE Leaders

skateboarding at an after-school club, community leadership by taking an active role in a local youth council or assisting with the local shopmobility scheme. They may also need to attend relevant meetings, prepare resources or help to organise an event.

4. Assessment – completing the section

At this stage the participant meets their Assessor to discuss and record their experiences, how they developed and reached their goals. As their DofE Leader you should help to organise this meeting or you may be doing this role yourself.

Additional areas that will need discussing and writing in the participant's *Record Book* are:
- Positive experiences and adventures they had along the way.

- How they felt at the beginning and the end.
- What they gained from it personally (think soft skills like teamwork, communication, planning).
- Any difficulties they faced and how they overcame them.

Don't forget that a participant's *Record Book* must be completed and signed by their Assessor and the participant to prove they have successfully completed this part of their programme.

If you are not their Assessor, then organise a final meeting with your participant to review their experience and achievements.

What can young people volunteer to do?

The list of types of volunteering and examples of activities shown overleaf should help you to point participants in the right direction when they're selecting their volunteering activity. Remember, activities can be undertaken on an individual or group basis.

Guidance notes are available to download at ***www.DofE.org/volunteering***

Volunteering section ideas

For this section, participants need to identify a need which they wish to help with and then see which of the categories below it fits into. They then need to plan what they can do to help and create their programme to meet this need. Listed in each category are examples of programmes that participants could do.

Helping people
Examples:
- Supporting a local primary school with their reading scheme.
- Being a DJ in their local youth club.
- Being a weekly visitor to an older person.
- Being a Listener for the Samaritans in a prison.
- Helping at an after-school club for kids with cerebral palsy.

Community action and raising awareness
Examples:
- Running a web campaign for their college to raise awareness of the issues around poverty in the world.

- Being an active member of Streetcred, the Youth Opportunities and Capital Fund for Bedfordshire.
- Running a campaign in their local faith group reminding people to register as an organ donor.
- Running a crime prevention project in their school with the local police.
- Being an active member of a youth council or forum.

Coaching, teaching and leadership
Examples:
- Being a DofE Leader.
- Being a uniformed youth group leader.
- Teaching numeracy to year six pupils.
- Being a football coach.
- Helping to coach their school's swimming team.

Working with the environment or animals
Examples:
- Helping with a local canal conservation project.
- Running a recycling project in their ATC Squadron.
- Doing a litter picking project for a local housing estate or park.
- Helping at a Cats Protection adoption centre.
- Running a campaign to stop people wasting energy.

Helping a charity or community organisation
Examples:
- Raising money for a cancer charity.
- Working in a charity shop.
- Being a trustee for a local charity.
- Helping with religious education classes.
- Decorating/doing up their Sea Cadet Unit's Headquarters.

> *"Helping the children at school gave me a real buzz as I knew I was also helping my community."*
> *Thomas, DofE participant*

Physical

Physical

Aim

To inspire young people to achieve greater physical fitness and a healthy lifestyle through participation and improvement in physical activity. From hockey to dance, rock climbing to swimming, wheelchair basketball to yoga – almost any dance, sport or fitness activity can count.

Principles

- Involvement in some form of enjoyable physical activity is essential for young people's physical health.
- Maintaining physical health is important to mental and emotional well-being.
- A lasting sense of achievement and satisfaction is derived from meeting a physical challenge.
- Physical activities are enjoyable in themselves and can lead to the establishment of a lasting, active lifestyle.

Benefits

Through doing physical activities, young people will:
- Enjoy keeping fit by choosing an activity which they enjoy.
- Improve fitness by taking part in a physical activity on a regular basis.
- Discover new abilities.
- Raise self-esteem through improvement of performance.
- Extend personal goals by involvement and sustained interest.
- Set and respond to a challenge by extending physical fitness and performance.
- Experience a sense of achievement from meeting a physical challenge.

So what is a physical activity?

In short, anything that requires a sustained level of physical energy and involves doing an activity. For example, playing a sport regularly and showing personal improvement would count. However, learning to become a coach in the same sport would be a Skills section activity, whilst being a volunteer coach counts for the Volunteering section.

Participants must choose a physical activity and with your help set an appropriate challenge. They can choose one they are currently doing or go for something new. The key is to show progression and sustained interest over time. Ultimately, participants must prove that they have broadened their understanding and increased their expertise in their chosen activity.

If your participant is unsure which category an activity falls into, or whether it's acceptable, they must get approval from you, your DofE Co-ordinator and your OA before starting. Generally this will be relatively straightforward if the activity has a national governing body or if it is recognised by UK Sport, the Central Council of Physical Recreation or the relevant Sports Council.

Helping young people to make the right choice

They don't need to be an Olympic athlete, pro-footballer or prima ballerina to achieve in the Physical section.

This flowchart gives a simple overview of the steps involved for a young person to complete their Physical section. Each step is explained in more detail on the following pages.

Preparation

Young people plan their physical activity and set their objectives.
This includes what sport, dance or fitness activity they want to do,
where they'll do it and for how long.

↓

Training

Participants undergo any training or briefing necessary to allow them to
undertake their physical activities. Training may form part of the activity.

↓

Activity

Participants do their physical activity regularly, averaging
at least an hour a week, for the planned time.

↓

Assessment

The young person meets with their Assessor, to discuss and record their
experiences, including their effort, perseverance and achievement.
Their *Record Book* is completed.

The Handbook for D*of*E Leaders

The key here is to have fun and become better and fitter. From wheelchair users who've learnt to scuba dive to nervous teenagers who've joined an aerobics class, from inner-city young women who've set up their own football team to young offenders who've built self-esteem through gym work – achievement is possible regardless of a young person's starting point or physical ability.

As a DofE Leader you must ensure that a participant's choice:
- Focuses on one specific theme or activity.
- Enables Assessors to easily measure progression over a period of time.
- Is undertaken in accordance with appropriate safe working practices and legal requirements.
- Is usually done in their own time.
- Reflects their individual interests, talents and capabilities.

Participants are free to do this section independently or as part of a team. To help set a 'benchmark' for monitoring and assessing progress, encourage them to go for a national governing body standard or award where appropriate.

The four steps to completing the Physical section

1. Preparation is everything
During their first meeting with you, or a nominated volunteer, the young person must agree their activity and set objectives. These should be tailored to their level of experience in the activity. Additionally this meeting must cover:
- What they plan to do, i.e. the practical activity, commitment required and its benefits.
- The starting point for the participant, recognising their current knowledge and personal ability.
- The agreed programme incorporating individual goals and ambitions.
- Any necessary safety or legal requirements.
- Whether they require support or training related to health and safety, skills and awareness.
- The process for evaluation and assessment, *see step four*.
- How progress is to be recorded and the format of the final review.
- The dates and times of meetings.

Timescales: Physical

Level	Minimum time	Notes
Bronze	3 or 6 months	*Young people must do one of their Volunteering, Physical or Skills sections for 6 months, the others for 3.*
Silver	3, 6 or 12 months	*Either the Physical or Skills section must be done for 6 months, the other for 3. Young people who haven't achieved Bronze must extend their Volunteering or the longer of their Physical or Skills sections to 12 months.*
Gold	6, 12 or 18 months	*Either the Physical or Skills section must be done for 12 months, the other for 6. Young people who haven't achieved Silver must extend their Volunteering or the longer of their Physical or Skills sections to 18 months.*

Remember, young people must commit to regular activities averaging at least an hour a week during this time.

2. Training to develop their talents

In order to complete this section a participant may have to undertake some form of training or briefing, prior to starting or even during their activity. It could be one of their sectional objectives or, equally importantly, a health and safety requirement.

3. Activity, enabling physical talents to bloom

With the goals set, participants can get going with their chosen activity. On a regular basis they should meet with you, their Supervisor and/or their Assessor to:

- Discuss progress
- Obtain clarification and guidance
- Obtain help to resolve any problems
- Reflect on progress and learn from experience
- Reaffirm or set new goals and discuss expectations for the next phase
- If necessary, review their choice of activity.

4. Assessment, completing the section

A participant's effort, perseverance and achievement should be regularly assessed throughout their time on this

section. If applicable, their contribution to the planning, execution and completion of their team's activities and performance must also be examined.

Participants have completed this section when their Assessor is happy that:
- The minimum time requirements have been met.
- Genuine effort and individual progress have been made within the young person's capability.

Your participant, together with their Assessor, will discuss and record their experiences in their *Record Book*, along with:
- How they developed and achieved their goals.
- The difficulties they faced and how they overcame them.
- Their contribution to their team or group.

Other areas that should be considered during this final review are:
- Effort
- Application
- Technique
- Skill
- Tactics
- Improvement in fitness and achievement
- Knowledge of the relevant rules and safety regulations
- Quality of experience.

Once this has been completed the *Record Book* should be signed by the Assessor and participant. If you are not the Assessor, then organise a final meeting to review your participant's experience and achievements.

Guidance notes are available to download at
www.DofE.org/physical

Physical section ideas

For this section, participants need to identify a physical activity that they want to get involved in, or improve at, from any of the categories below. They then need to set themselves objectives and create their programme to meet them. Listed in each category are examples of programmes that participants could do.

Team sports
Examples:
- Joining a local football team and playing in matches regularly.
- Taking part in after-school hockey lessons.
- Learning the rules of ultimate flying disc and joining their college team.
- Joining their Girls' Brigade Company's netball team and playing in their league.
- Playing wheelchair basketball at their school.

Individual sports
Examples:
- Joining a local athletics club and competing for their area.

- Setting regular dates to go bowling with a group of friends.
- Learning to fence at a local community centre.
- Learning to horse ride at the local stables.
- Practicing rollerblading every week and joining in a open session in their local park.

Water sports
Examples:
- Learning to windsurf at a local lake.
- Gaining a PADI open water SCUBA diving qualification and going out on subsequent dives.
- Joining a local dragon boat racing team and competing at a regatta.
- Going swimming every week at the local pool.
- Learning to surf on holiday and continuing to practice at their local beach.

Racquet sports
Examples:
- Learning to play tennis in their lunchtime club at school.
- Playing badminton every week with friends.

- Playing table tennis regularly at their youth club.
- Joining a tennis club and playing in matches.
- Having squash lessons at their local gym.

Dance

Examples:
- Learning bhangra at a local dance studio.
- Attending salsa classes every week at the local community centre.
- Creating a street dance routine with friends for their District Scout Gang Show.
- Improving their ballet skills and gaining the next grade.
- Joining, and performing with, a local sword dancing team.

Fitness

Examples:
- Going to their local gym every week and improving cardiovascular fitness.
- Jogging or walking every week with friends.
- Doing an activity class, i.e. aerobics, pilates, yoga, at their local sports centre.
- Joining a trampolining club.
- Learning to weightlift in a prison gym and showing improvement.

Extreme sports

Examples:
- Mountain biking with friends and learning how to do jumps.
- Skateboarding regularly at their local skatepark.
- Joining a free running group.
- Improving their climbing ability at the local climbing wall.
- Learning how to skydive and doing two tandem jumps.

Martial arts

Examples:
- Improving their karate skills and gaining the next belt.
- Taking part in self-defence lessons at an after-school club.
- Joining tai-chi classes in their local park.
- Learning the skills of Capoeira at local classes.
- Joining a judo club at their local community centre.

Skills

Skills

Aim

To inspire young people to develop practical and social skills and personal interests. From podcasting to playing a musical instrument, fine art to website design, cookery to learning to drive, the sky's the limit!

Principles

- By choosing to develop a particular skill young people realise their unique potential and gain greater self-esteem.
- Everyone has the ability to learn. Young people should have the opportunity to develop skills.
- All young people have unique potential and should value themselves. Developing a skill will help them realise this.

Benefits

By learning a skill, participants will:
- Develop a new talent.
- Improve self-esteem and confidence.
- Develop practical and social skills — by working alongside enthusiastic individuals who share their skills and knowledge.
- Develop better organisational and time management skills.
- Sharpen research skills — by using libraries, the internet and the local community, they will have to identify and source help and guidance.
- Learn how to set and rise to a challenge.

Something old or something new – selecting a skill

Participants must choose an activity and with your help set an appropriate challenge. They can choose to improve an existing skill or develop a new one. The key is to show progression and sustained interest over time.

Ultimately, participants must be able to prove that they have broadened their understanding and increased their expertise of their chosen skill. Activities can be undertaken on either an individual or group basis.

Most DofE groups/centres are only able to offer a small selection of activities that count as a skill. If a young person wishes to try something else they can organise it themselves and check the details with you for approval. This must be done before they start.

Helping young people to make the right choice

As a DofE Leader you must ensure that a participant's choice:
- Focuses on one specific theme or activity.
- Enables their Assessor to easily measure progression over a period of time.
- Is undertaken in accordance with appropriate safe working practices and legal requirements.
- Is normally done in their own time.
- Reflects their individual interests, talents and capabilities.

This flowchart gives a simple overview of the steps involved for a young person to complete their Skills section. Each step is explained in more detail on the following pages.

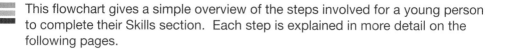

Preparation

Young people choose to improve an existing skill or develop a new one. They research their choice, plan what to do, how long for and set their objectives.

↓

Training

Participants undergo any training necessary to allow them to undertake their skills activity. The skill chosen could be a course, in which case training will be the full activity.

↓

Activity

Participants undertake their skills activity – learning by doing regularly, averaging at least an hour a week, for the planned time.

↓

Assessment

The young person meets with their Assessor to discuss and record their experiences, what they learnt and how they met their goals. Their *Record Book* is completed.

The Handbook for *DofE* Leaders

- The starting point for the participant, recognising their current knowledge and personal ability.
- The agreed programme incorporating individual goals and ambitions.
- Any necessary safety or legal requirements.
- Support or training related to health and safety, skills and awareness.
- How progress is to be recorded and the format of the final review.
- The dates and times of meetings.

The start date for this section is your meeting and the finish date will be when the skill has been fully assessed and the *Record Book* completed.

The four steps to completing the Skills section

1. Preparation is everything

It's vital that the participant researches their chosen activity thoroughly prior to meeting with you to discuss their choice. This will enable them to discuss constructively what personal goals should be set. During the meeting you must cover:

- The process for evaluation and assessment.
- The activity to be pursued i.e. the practical task, commitment required and the benefits to the participant.

2. Training to develop their talents

Development of a skill is often a combination of training and practical activity. For some activities, initial training may be required so that young people are safe to do the work, whereas for others, the skill chosen could be a course and it will be the full activity. If this is the case, it is likely that the adult doing their training will also be their Assessor.

Timescales: Skills

Level	Minimum time	Notes
Bronze	3 or 6 months	*Young people must do one of their Volunteering, Physical or Skills sections for 6 months, the others for 3.*
Silver	3, 6 or 12 months	*Either the Physical or Skills section must be done for 6 months, the other for 3. Young people who haven't achieved Bronze must extend their Volunteering or the longer of their Physical or Skills sections to 12 months.*
Gold	6, 12 or 18 months	*Either the Physical or Skills section must be done for 12 months, the other for 6. Young people who haven't achieved Silver must extend their Volunteering or the longer of their Physical or Skills sections to 18 months.*

Remember, young people must commit to regular activities averaging at least an hour a week during this time.

3. Activity, enabling talents to bloom

Participants learn by doing their programme. Therefore ongoing support through meetings with you, their Assessor and/or Supervisor is crucial. During these meetings it is important to:

- Discuss progress
- Clarify and provide guidance
- Help to resolve any problems
- Reflect on progress and learn from experience
- Reaffirm or set new goals and discuss expectations for the next phase
- If necessary, review the choice of activity.

4. Assessment, completing the section

All participants should be regularly assessed to check their effort, perseverance and achievement. Their contribution to the planning, execution and completion of group activities will also fall under the spotlight.

Participants have completed this section when their Assessor is happy that:

- The skill has been regularly followed for the required time.
- Genuine effort and individual progress have been made within the young person's capability.

Your participant, with their Assessor, will discuss and record their experiences in their *Record Book*, along with:
- How they developed and their progress towards achieving the objectives they set.
- Difficulties faced and how they overcame them.

Once this has been completed the *Record Book* should be signed by the Assessor and participant.

If you are not the Assessor, then organise a final meeting to review your participant's experience and achievements.

*Guidance notes are available to download at **www.DofE.org/skills***

Skills section ideas

For this section, participants need to identify a skills activity that they want to learn, or improve at, from any of the categories below. They then need to set themselves objectives and create their programme to meet them. Listed in each category are examples of programmes that participants could do.

Creative arts
Examples:
- Learning how to knit and making a piece of clothing.
- Taking a jewellery making course at their college.
- Learning how to cook food from different countries at their local youth group.
- Doing art classes at a local centre and taking part in an exhibition.
- Going to pottery classes at a local pottery café and creating a set of mugs.

Performance arts
Examples:
- Going to speech and drama classes at a local club.
- Singing in a school musical.
- Learning how to juggle.
- Teaching themselves how to do magic tricks and performing at a children's party.
- Improving their baton twirling skills at their majorettes club.

Science and technology
Examples:
- Taking part in an after-school experimental science club.
- Joining a local astronomy club.
- Teaching themselves a new computer software package.
- Learning about electronics and constructing a radio.
- Building microscope slides of plant and animal cells.

Care of animals
Examples:
- Learning about and keeping tropical fish.
- Helping a local beekeeper at the weekends and tasting the honey created.
- Taking their dog to obedience classes.
- Feeding animals at their local farm and learning key handling skills.
- Mucking out horses and learning how to care for them.

Music
Examples:
- Learning to DJ and playing at friends' parties.
- Taking piano lessons and gaining a higher grade.
- Studying classical music and attending concerts.

The Handbook for *DofE* Leaders

- Joining the school choir.
- Playing the drums in a band with their mates and holding a gig for family and friends.

- Joining their university debating society.
- Producing and distributing a newsletter for their youth group.

Life skills
Examples:
- Learning about interview and CV-writing techniques with a local business.
- Undertaking a first aid course with their St. John Ambulance Group.
- Learning to type and gaining an award.
- Learning how to drive and being able to demonstrate basic car maintenance.
- Being an active member of a Young Enterprise group at their college.

Learning and collecting
Examples:
- Learning about different cloud formations and giving a presentation to their youth group.
- Learning about different birds and going on bird watching trips with friends.
- Collecting stamps from a range of eras and cataloguing them.
- Studying geology and collecting different rock types.
- Compiling a book on the fashions of the last decade.

Media and communication
Examples:
- Learning about today's digital lifestyle, creating a video clip and posting it online.
- Taking a writing course and publishing an article in the Boys' Brigade magazine.
- Learning British Sign Language.

Natural world
Examples:
- Studying orchids and successfully growing a selection.
- Maintaining a pond in their garden and studying pond life.
- Growing vegetables on an allotment and entering them in the village fete.
- Learning about conservation and environmental work through after-school classes.
- Studying groundsmanship by shadowing a local groundskeeper at a football club.

Games and sports
Examples:
- Joining a local snooker club and playing in the league.
- Taking part in an after-school chess club.
- Being taught how to fish on a local river by a family friend.
- Learning how to go-kart at a local track.
- Studying and constructing a kite and flying it at a youth festival.

Expedition

Expedition

Aim

To inspire young people to develop initiative and a spirit of adventure and discovery, by planning, training for and completing an adventurous journey as part of a team. From cycling in the Galloway Hills, walking in the Brecon Beacons or canoeing down the Thames to sailing in the Mediterranean, horse riding in Chile or walking in the Alps, the expedition can be as far flung or as close to home as participants want it to be.

Principles

- Participation in shared experiences in the outdoor environment can develop initiative, teamwork, communication, leadership, problem solving and organisational skills.
- Experiencing and overcoming challenges together develops emotional strength and empathy for others.

Benefits

Through participation in an expedition young people:
- Gain an appreciation of and respect for the outdoor environment.
- Learn the value of sharing responsibility for success, through leadership, teamwork, self-reliance and co-operation.
- Learn the importance of attention to detail and organisational ability.
- Develop and demonstrate enterprise and imagination.
- Become more self-reliant.

- Become more able to overcome both expected and unexpected challenges.
- Recognise the needs and strengths of others.
- Improve decision-making skills and the ability to accept consequences.
- Gain the skills to reflect on personal performance.
- Learn to manage risk.
- Learn through experience.

What is involved?

The Expedition section involves planning, training for and completing an unaccompanied, self-reliant expedition with an agreed aim.

All participants must do at least one practice expedition and a qualifying expedition (the one that is assessed) in order to complete the section.

Expeditions must be completed by the participants' own physical efforts with minimal external intervention and without motorised assistance. The route should be a continuous journey.

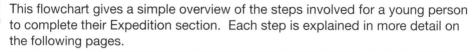

This flowchart gives a simple overview of the steps involved for a young person to complete their Expedition section. Each step is explained in more detail on the following pages.

Preparation

Participants plan an expedition. This includes team members, its aim, how they will travel and the environment they intend to travel through. Expeditions may be undertaken by foot, bicycle, sailboat, canoe, kayak, wheelchair or on horseback.

↓

Training

Participants undergo training in expedition skills and their chosen mode of travel.

↓

Practice expedition

Participants must undertake sufficient practice expeditions to enable them to travel safely and complete their qualifying expedition.

↓

Qualifying expedition, debrief and presentation

Once prepared, participants undertake their expedition, which will be observed by their accredited Assessor. On completion they will be debriefed by their Assessor and then prepare and give a presentation of their expedition which covers their aims, experiences and outcomes.

↓

Assessment

Their *Record Book* is completed by their Assessor following the qualifying expedition and also by the person who saw their presentation.

Preparation is everything

First, participants should decide on their expedition team. There must be between four and seven young people in a team (eight for modes of travel which can be used by two people at once, e.g. tandem bikes, open canoes). Many DofE groups will have more participants than the number required for just one team and you may need to help them work out who will be in each team. Teams can be chosen in many ways: friendship groups, shared choice of aim/location or skills in a particular mode of travel etc.

With teams in place, young people need to decide on the nature of the expedition that they wish to undertake. They must first consider what they want their aim to be, then the location and mode of travel. The expedition's aim should relate to the interests and abilities of those taking part and the area they will be travelling through. This is the key to any expedition's success. Without it, they can't plan an effective, challenging expedition with a clear outcome – simply travelling through the countryside is not enough. Some examples of aims could include:

- A piece of work related to the environment they're travelling through,

for example, examining footpath erosion or studying the local wildlife.
- A physically demanding expedition – for example, young people may want to challenge themselves by walking for the full amount of hours every day.
- Use canoes to explore and research historical buildings on a lake system.
- Examining group dynamics and team working.

It is worth reminding your participants at this time that their post-qualifying expedition presentation will be based on this aim and is the result of their own observations during their expedition. Once their aim is set, it will help to choose an appropriate environment in which to do their expedition. It will also provide a guide as to the amount of time a team will spend travelling or exploring.

Finally, working with you and/or their Supervisor, the team should choose their mode of travel. This should be suitable for the aim and location, something they have the skills to do (or will learn to do) and that they will find enjoyable.

With all this in place, you can agree with your team(s) their training plan and dates of practice and qualifying expeditions.

Training to develop their knowledge

Safety is paramount when it comes to the expedition. Therefore, it is essential that participants undertake expedition skills training using the DofE's Expedition Training Framework.

This provides a structure for training young people undertaking their Expedition section. Using it can help prepare young people to meet the challenges of their expedition.

There are additional guidelines to assist with specific modes of travel, such as the paddle expeditions document, available at **www.DofE.org/training**

The Expedition Training Framework covers:
- First aid and emergency procedures
- An awareness of risk and health and safety issues
- Navigation and route planning
- Campcraft, equipment and hygiene
- Food and cooking
- Countryside, Highway and Water Sports Codes (as appropriate)
- Observation and recording
- Team building
- Proficiency in the mode of travel.

You can read the detailed Expedition Training Framework in the *Expedition Guide* and at **www.DofE.org/training**

EX² (our interactive expedition training tool) also contains further details along with practical advice and training support. This is available from our shop at **www.DofE.org/shop**

Practice expedition(s)

Both enjoyable and essential, practice expedition(s) must closely replicate the conditions of the actual expedition. This includes equivalent daily hours of journeying, mode of travel, accommodation and terrain. Participants must undertake at least one practice expedition at each level.

The team's Supervisor must continually assess the competence and confidence of the expedition team and, if necessary, help them to undertake additional training and practices.

Never forget that you and their Supervisor must be confident that they will be able to safely complete their qualifying expedition unaccompanied. As their Supervisor gains greater confidence in the team's abilities, they can reduce their level of close supervision enabling the team to undertake unaccompanied journeys prior to going on the qualifying expedition. If you are not the Supervisor, you should keep in regular contact with them to ensure you are happy with their progress.

Silver and Gold practices must include at least two consecutive nights away. At Gold level at least one practice must be in an appropriate environment similar to that of the proposed qualifying expedition. For expeditions on land this should be in a designated wild country area.

Activity, qualifying expedition and debrief

The team should plan how they spend their time to complete their expedition and meet their aim.

It is crucial that the speed of journeying, the distance travelled and the time spent exploring is determined by the team to meet their individual needs. Experienced DofE Leaders and Supervisors will enable young people to choose a sufficiently challenging combination of journeying and exploring. This should be based on their experiences during practice expeditions in a similar environment.

A good team can work out average distances based on their training and practice expeditions.

Timescales for qualifying expeditions		
Level	**Duration**	**Minimum hours of planned activity each day**
Bronze	2 days and 1 night	At least 6 hours during the daytime (at least 3 of which must be spent journeying)
Silver	3 days and 2 nights	At least 7 hours during the daytime (at least 3½ of which must be spent journeying)
Gold	4 days and 3 nights	At least 8 hours during the daytime (at least 4 of which must be spent journeying)

Time associated with overnight accommodation and catering is additional to the minimum daytime hours of planned activity.

The Handbook for *DofE* Leaders

Recommended Environments

Bronze*	
Land Environment (walking, cycling and horse riding)	Normal rural countryside which can be familiar to the participants.
Canoeing and Rowing	Canals, rivers or other inland waterways and lakes.
Sailing	Inland waters or sheltered estuaries well within the participants' competencies.

Silver*	
Land Environment (walking, cycling and horse riding)	Normal rural, open countryside or forest, which is unfamiliar to the participants. The environment should be more demanding for participants than at Bronze level. Where possible the expedition should all be in, or at least include, areas of open country or forest.
Canoeing and Rowing	Canals, rivers or other inland waterways and lakes in rural areas.
Sailing	Inland waters, estuaries or sheltered coastal waters.

Gold	
Land Environment (walking, cycling and horse riding)	Wild country** (remote from habitation) which is unfamiliar to participants. The environment should be more demanding for participants than at Silver level. Remote estuaries, marshes, fens and coastal areas may provide an appropriate environment for an expedition with the emphasis on exploring rather than doing the journey.
Canoeing and Rowing	Rivers or other inland waterways and lakes in rural areas, sheltered coastal waters or estuaries.
Sailing	Inland waters, estuaries or sheltered coastal waters. Yachts may be used in open sea areas.

Where Bronze and Silver expeditions are proposed in surroundings more demanding than those recommended, participants must be trained and equipped to enable them to meet any potential hazards. You should use the DofE Expedition Training Framework for the Silver or Gold levels.

** *Wild country is defined as an area remote from habitation. DofE expeditions should be through, rather than over, wild country – it's all about solitude not altitude.*

A map of UK wild country areas can be found at **www.DofE.org/expedition** Each area has a DofE Expedition Co-ordinator and a network of experienced volunteers able to assess teams and provide local expedition advice. The contact details of all the Expedition Co-ordinators are available from DofE Regional/Country Offices and on our website **www.DofE.org/expedition**

Equipment

Teams should carry all their equipment and food to enable them to operate in a self-sufficient way. However, there may be some cases when a participant has special needs or circumstances that make it inappropriate for them to carry full camping and cooking equipment and it cannot be carried by the rest of the team. In these cases only, some items may be deposited at the camp sites or agreed check points.

Each individual must carry the personal emergency equipment as listed on our website.

Accommodation

Participants should stop at different locations each night and only use the same camp site when necessary to meet their aim. Teams should still travel to and from the camp site as part of their journeying.

Light-weight camping enhances the sense of adventure and self-reliance. However, on rare occasions to take into account the needs of participants, alternative basic types of accommodation may be considered.

Preparing for a wild country expedition

If teams are intending to travel unaccompanied through wild country areas and need an Assessor, an expedition notification form *(Green Form)* must be completed and forwarded at least six weeks in advance to the relevant DofE Expedition Co-ordinator.

Find out where to send them at **www.DofE.org/expedition** or from the DofE Regional/Country Office.

If your Operating Authority already has an Accredited Assessor and doesn't need one from the Assessor network, send your *Green Form* four weeks in advance. These forms are available from your Operating Authority, our website (**www.DofE.org**) and DofE Regional/Country Offices.

Wild country expeditions are exciting but it's important that the team is fully prepared for the environment and know how to use their equipment.

Participants should always arrive the day before the start of the expedition. This way the entire team and the Supervisor can meet the Assessor and make an early start. At Gold, the team should set aside an acclimatisation day before the expedition in order to get used to the environment. To enhance the experience, the base camp site should not be used by the team as the expedition camp site.

Assessment

Qualifying expeditions must be assessed by an accredited Assessor *(see page 76)*. During the expedition the Assessor will meet with the team at various agreed times to check on progress.

Following the qualifying expedition and debrief the Assessor completes the section on the expedition in the *Record Book*. The team then give a presentation. All relevant details must also be entered by the adult that the

team presented to after the presentation and final review. Participants should be encouraged to add their own comments.

Debrief

Whilst the team will be tired and very excited, make sure the Assessor conducts a full debrief immediately after the expedition is completed (on the final day). During this meeting everyone should participate in reviewing the outcomes of the expedition.

After the debrief it is important to give participants time to reflect on their expedition and its aims. This will enable the team to prepare and deliver a presentation of their experiences.

Presentation

It is entirely up to the team how their presentation is delivered – it could be photographic, an online blog, audio visual, dramatic etc. With your agreement, they can also choose who they want to present it to. It could be you, their Supervisor, their Assessor or another suitable adult.

The 20 conditions of the Expedition section

	DofE Qualifying Expedition Conditions	Further explanation and interpretation of conditions
1	All expeditions must be by the participants' own physical effort, without motorised or outside assistance.	
2	All expeditions must be unaccompanied and self-sufficient.	a) The team must be unaccompanied, unguided and supervision must be carried out remotely. b) As part of effective remote supervision, teams may be more closely supervised for parts of the expedition where specific hazards are unavoidable. This supervision should be kept to an absolute minimum. c) If a team does not possess the necessary expedition and medical skills required for an area, then they should not be in that area.
3	All expeditions must be supervised by an adult who is able to accept responsibility for the safety of the team.	
4	The expedition must have an aim.	
5	All participants must be properly equipped.	
6	Participants must have completed the required training and practice expeditions.	The qualifying expedition must not be over the same route or in the immediate vicinity of routes used in practice expeditions.
7	At least one practice expedition must be undertaken at each level of the programme, in the same mode of travel in a similar environment to the qualifying expedition.	For overseas assessed expeditions, at least one UK practice must have taken place in an appropriate environment.
8	The team must plan and organise the expedition.	Multiple teams should not travel in convoy but have individual routes from camp site to camp site. Where this is unavoidable at least 30 minutes must separate each team using the same route and they must operate as discrete teams.
9	Assessment must be by an approved accredited Assessor.	

The Handbook for DofE Leaders

10	There must be between four and seven in a team (eight for modes of travel which have tandem).	
11	All participants must be within the qualifying age of the programme level.	This is regardless of whether they are under assessment or not.
12	Participants must be at the same level of assessment.	Participants should have a similar ability or level of experience and make a full contribution to the team.
13	The team must not include those who have completed the same or higher level expedition.	Participants should have a similar ability or level of experience and make a full contribution to the team.
14	Accommodation should be by camping.	
15	The expedition must be of the correct duration.	a) The expedition must be of the minimum number of days and nights and must include appropriate acclimatisation/final preparation time. b) An acclimatisation day during an expedition due to extreme altitude may be included as long as the minimum hours of activity and journeying are still completed. c) An additional acclimatisation/rest day may be included during an expedition but this will not count toward the expedition days.
16	The expedition should normally take place between the end of March and the end of October.	The expedition must take place at an appropriate time of year for the expedition's location and aim and the enjoyment of the participants.
17	The expedition should take place in the recommended environment.	The expedition should take place in an appropriate and challenging environment. Overseas expeditions should take place in an area appropriate to the level of the expedition.
18	The expedition must meet the minimum hours of planned activity.	a) Six hours at Bronze, seven hours at Silver and eight hours at Gold. At least half of these daily hours must be spent travelling. b) Time associated with overnight accommodation and catering is additional to the minimum daytime hours of planned activity.
19	A substantial meal should be cooked and eaten by participants each day.	This is optional on the final day.
20	A presentation must be prepared and delivered after the expedition.	The presentation or report, which may be in any format the participants choose, must be related to the expedition's aim and level.

Variations to the 20 conditions

Where participants have individual needs that mean one or more of the above conditions cannot be met, they may apply for a variation to enable them to complete their DofE expedition.

Variation application forms are available at **www.DofE.org/expedition** or from DofE Regional/Country Offices. At Bronze and Silver they must be approved through the participant's Operating Authority and at Gold through the appropriate DofE Regional/Country Office.

Written approval of these variations should be attached to the appropriate expedition notification form when submitted for approval. The application form must be sent in sufficient time to reach the relevant office at least 12 weeks prior to the date of departure.

Multiple teams

Some large DofE groups may have several expedition teams being assessed in the same area at the same time. The DofE strongly discourages multiple teams using the same expedition route. Multiple teams must always operate independently and discreetly. Where the use of the same route is unavoidable, usually due to the expedition environment, for example canoe expeditions, rather than the availability of Supervisors, then the teams must be separated by at least 30 minutes journeying time. Teams should take it in turns to be the lead team on different expeditioning days.

Expeditions outside the United Kingdom

All Expedition section conditions apply equally to expeditions taking place

The Handbook for DofE Leaders

outside the United Kingdom. In addition all participants must complete at least one practice expedition in the UK before departure.

Notice must be given to the Operating Authority at least 12 weeks in advance, using the standard notification form for expeditions abroad *(Blue Form)* which you can download at **www.DofE.org** The expedition provider, whether this is you or an organisation you have brought in to help, must accept responsibility for monitoring the safety of the expedition. This must be done in accordance with the policies and guidelines of your Operating Authority.

If accepted by your OA, your DofE Regional/Country Office will provide you with a notification reference number, which must be entered in the participants' *Record Books* on successful completion of the expedition.

The team should notify the country's National Award Authority, if the DofE programme operates in the country the team is planning to visit. This can be done at the International Award's website **www.intaward.org**

Adventurous projects

There may be times when a team plans an expedition that is adventurous and challenging but due to its very specific nature it might not be possible to meet one or two of the 20 conditions of the Expedition section.

In this case these expeditions will be assessed by the DofE Head Office to see if 'adventurous project' status can be granted. These projects will be one-off expeditions in the UK or overseas and can only be used by participants over the age of 16. They can be used for any DofE programme level.

Some conditions, such as the need for the team to be unaccompanied or for an appropriate practice expedition to be completed, are not flexible but other conditions may have some flexibility.

Teams who believe that their expedition may qualify as an adventurous project should seek the guidance of their DofE Manager at least six months prior to the expedition and before they have committed to any expenditure.

Before making a formal application, participants must read the relevant advice in the *Expedition Guide* or on EX². Adventurous project application forms are available at **www.DofE.org/expedition** or from DofE Regional/Country Offices. These must be completed and attached to the appropriate notification form when submitted. These forms must arrive at the DofE Head Office at least 12 weeks prior to the date of departure.

An adventurous project reference number will be allocated to each approved expedition and should be entered in the participants' *Record Books* on successful completion.

Note: In giving approval for such expeditions, The Duke of Edinburgh's Award only confirms that the expedition complies with the aim, principles and purpose of the Expedition section. We do not accept responsibility for health and safety and public liability insurance. This rests with you or the activity provider approved by your Operating Authority.

Safety

Operating Authorities are responsible for the safety and well-being of all participants. They also approve Supervisors and Assessors and set training, experience and/or qualifications that are required. As a DofE Leader you must ensure that all your OA's requirements are fulfilled. Whilst we do not insist on specific qualifications it is strongly recommended that suitable national qualifications for the chosen modes of travel are obtained.

You, or your chosen expedition activity provider, are responsible for the suitability of expeditions, safety aspects, the adequacy of the training and emergency procedures. If this is not your OA, then they should ensure that the activity provider is reputable, risks have been assessed and that Supervisors and Assessors are suitably competent.

Specific, detailed advice on training, supervision and assessment can be found in the *Expedition Guide* or on EX².

We'll now outline additional responsibilities for adults involved in the Expedition section. *These are in addition to the overall responsibilities stated in chapter two.*

Expedition Supervisors

All expeditions, including practice expeditions, must be supervised by a suitably experienced adult who is competent in the chosen mode of travel. Additionally, Supervisors should be familiar with the team, their individual strengths and weaknesses and their knowledge of the chosen route. An understanding of the aims, principles and requirements of the Expedition section is also essential.

Supervisors accept responsibility for the safety and welfare of the team on behalf of the OA. They must be satisfied that participants are capable of undertaking the planned expedition. This is important as the qualifying expedition is unaccompanied. Contact with adults should be kept to a minimum.

The Supervisor, if you are not undertaking this role, may help you arrange training for the team in the DofE Expedition Training Framework which is outlined in the *Expedition Guide* and at **www.DofE.org/expedition** Training should only be provided by those who have the necessary skills and experience and are approved by your Operating Authority.

Whilst expeditions are conducted unaccompanied and supervised remotely, Supervisors must always be able to deal with team emergencies.

In wild country or at sea, coast and remote areas of marshland, the Supervisor must be based in the area where the expedition takes place. Expeditions in estuaries or sheltered

coastal waters may be supervised from a safety boat. However, they must maintain a sufficient distance from the participants so that they maintain their self-reliance, yet be able to give assistance quickly in an emergency. For expeditions at sea in larger craft designed to accommodate the whole team, the Supervisor and Assessor should not be involved in the skippering, crewing, navigation, control or management of the boat, except in an emergency for reasons of safety.

Supervisors may supervise teams more closely for short periods of an expedition when travelling through dangerous environments. This must be kept to an absolute minimum and used to allow a team to overcome an unavoidable dangerous area in their expedition route.

For the vast majority, if the team does not have the necessary training and skills to operate safely in an area unaccompanied for the duration of the expedition, then they should not be in that environment.

All relevant safety information must be carried by Supervisors. This includes the names, addresses and emergency contact numbers for participants, the Assessor, a nominated person in the OA and the DofE's Head Office emergency telephone number.

Expedition Assessors

All qualifying expeditions must be assessed by a competent adult who is approved by your Operating Authority and accredited by The Duke of Edinburgh's Award.

The role of the Assessor is to:
- Ensure that the aim of the Expedition section is met.
- Ensure that the conditions of the Expedition section are fulfilled. *Assessors are the guardians of the DofE's high standards.*
- Assist with the safety of the participants, by advising them on their route, equipment etc. *Responsibility for the health and safety of the team rests entirely with the Supervisor. The Expedition Supervisor is the representative of the Operating Authority, responsible for the safety and the welfare of the participants whilst on the expedition. If there are serious safety concerns, as a last resort, Assessors can withdraw their services, which will bring the assessment of the expedition to an end.*
- Protect the interests of the DofE. *The Assessor represents the DofE's interests in the area. This is largely achieved by using local knowledge to avoid sensitive areas and friction with certain landowners or overburdened communities.*

All Expedition Assessors must be accredited at the appropriate level through The Duke of Edinburgh's Award Expedition Assessor Accreditation Scheme. For details contact your OA, DofE Regional/Country Office or visit our website: **www.DofE.org/training**

Please note:
- At Bronze and Silver level, Assessors should not have been involved in any training or instruction of the team.
- At Gold level, the Assessor must be independent of your DofE group and not associated with the team in any way.

Open Expeditions

These enable independent participants, those who missed their own group's expedition or those unable to form a viable team, to complete practice and qualifying expeditions. They include a familiarisation and planning period followed by a supervised and assessed expedition. All necessary training and practice expeditions must be undertaken before a participant can take part in an open qualifying expedition.

Open opportunities are advertised at **www.DofE.org/opportunities**

Approved Activity Providers

We appreciate that not all DofE Leaders want, or are able, to lead expeditions.

We approve some organisations to deliver training, practice and qualifying expeditions to help groups complete their Expedition section.

See chapter six, page 105 for further information.

Supporting publications and materials

- Our website contains useful information including details of the Expedition Training Framework for each level of DofE programme (**www.DofE.org/expedition**), the notification forms and information about a number of expedition areas.
- Participants, Supervisors and Assessors should use EX² interactive training and the *Expedition Guide* as source materials and as a basis for their training programmes.
- Other important information is produced by government departments, relevant national governing bodies, The British Sports Trust and many environmental and conservation organisations.

Expedition section ideas

For this section, participants need to identify their expedition aim, mode of travel and location. Listed in each category are examples of expeditions that participants could do.

By foot

Examples:

- Exploring team dynamics and skills with a different team leader each day as they explore the Cairngorms.
- Conducting a study of insects on the South Downs.
- Planning a route in the Lake District to visit areas that inspired three of Wordsworth's poems.
- Considering the impact of tourism on the flora, fauna and wildlife of the French Alps.
- Following a series of footpaths in the Mourne Mountains, taking photographs to illustrate the Countryside Code to other DofE participants.

By bicycle

Examples:

- Investigating features of the Thames using the Thames Cycle Path.
- Following part of Gerald of Wales's route of 1188 through Pembrokeshire.
- Undertaking a physically demanding expedition in the Cheviot Hills.
- Using the cycle system in the Netherlands to undertake a research project on the provision and quality of cycle paths compared to the UK.
- Exploring 'Constable Country' in Suffolk, visiting places where Constable painted and taking photographs of the current landscape to compare the scenes with the paintings.

By boat

Examples:

- Exploring the Norfolk Broads using sailing dinghies.
- Planning a cross channel journey in a yacht.
- On their expedition, using simple mapping techniques to produce their own map of a local estuary and comparing it with a professional map when they return.
- Rowing along the Danube in Germany booking camp sites in advance.
- Planning a Bronze sailing expedition on Lake Ullswater in the Lake District.

By canoe or kayak

Examples:

- Recording the wildlife found on the Strangford Lough canoe trail.
- Taking a series of photos to come up with a guide to a section of London canal systems.
- Making a study of the locks and lochs on the Caledonian canal.
- Carrying out a wilderness trip in Canada utilising the canoe trails used by the original settlers.
- Choosing several points along a river and measuring speed of flow, width and depth. Comparing the differences along their route, trying to explain why this may be.

By wheelchair

Examples:

- Following a disused railway track noting the current use of previous railway buildings.
- Producing an illustrated guide to a stretch of canal. Researching the history and then travelling along the tow path using the expedition to gather photographs and sketches to illustrate the guide.

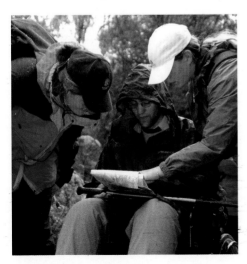

- Planning a route in Cropton Forest to take a series of landscape photographs to use in a calendar.
- Preparing a users guide of a country park or National Trust estate, explaining how it can be used, e.g. fishing, picnicking, conservation.
- Planning and undertaking a challenging route in the Peak District, making a short video diary of their experiences.

On horseback

Examples:

- Planning an expedition on horseback in the countryside including identifying suitable farm camp sites and bridleways.
- Planning an expedition with sea views in Devon, taking photos along the way so that they can paint a picture of their favourite scene when they return.
- Exploring accessibility and bridle paths in the Brecon Beacons.
- Going on an expedition through wooded areas, noting the different types of trees and age of trees they observe along the way.
- Going on a horse-riding expedition and writing a poem on their return to describe their experiences.

Residential

Residential (Gold level only)

Aim

To inspire participants through a concentrated involvement with people they don't know, who are usually from different backgrounds, and bring alternative views to the challenges they will face. The Residential section broadens their experiences by empowering them to make a difference in a team-based residential setting.

The powerful positive impact on a young person of a well structured residential experience is widely acknowledged. For the DofE this is a fundamental element of Gold DofE programmes, often providing the most important transformational experience for those involved.

Participants could base their experience around an existing interest, for example taking part in a sailing course, developing their photography skills or working on a conservation project. Alternatively they could try something completely new – like working at a kids' summer camp, learning French in Paris or helping to rebuild a school in the Gambia.

Principles

- Residential experiences take young people outside their normal environment and enable them to separate themselves from their daily routine.
- It is a chance to step outside their comfort zone, gain new skills for life, enjoy new experiences and have fun.
- By finding opportunities that interest them away from their usual group of friends, they will develop initiative and planning skills.
- By taking part in a residential, young people will broaden their horizons and develop maturity and independence.
- Interaction with people from different walks of life, ages and backgrounds promotes respect and understanding.
- Completion of shared objectives will develop social and teamworking skills and better prepare them for adulthood.

Benefits

Through completing the Residential section, young people will:
- Meet people.
- Develop the confidence to thrive in an unfamiliar environment.
- Build new relationships and show concern for others.
- Work as part of a team towards shared goals.
- Accept responsibility for themselves and others.
- Develop communication skills and effective coping mechanisms.
- Develop respect and understanding for others.
- Show initiative.
- Develop the skills and attitudes to live and work with others.

What is required?

Participants undertake a shared activity or specific course with people they don't know in a residential setting away from home and in an unfamiliar environment. Evenings are often as much a part of the experience as the daytime activities.

This flowchart gives a simple overview of the steps involved for a young person to complete their Residential section. Each step is explained in more detail on the following pages.

Preparation

Young people identify a residential activity they're interested in doing, where it's taking place and who they'll do it with. They'll set themselves personal goals and let the activity provider know they want their participation to count for their DofE programme.

Training

Participants undergo any training/preparation necessary to allow them to take part in the residential.

Activity

Participants join their residential and take part in the activities for a minimum of five days and four nights.

Assessment

At the end of the residential activity, the young person meets with their Assessor to discuss, record and review the quality of their experience.
Their *Record Book* is completed.

In order to give participants every chance of contributing to activities and gaining real benefit, they will usually require briefing or training prior to starting their residential activity.

How long for

The residential activity should normally take place over at least five consecutive days with a minimum of four nights spent away. In exceptional circumstances, and at the discretion of the OA, this commitment can be spread over two weekends. However, it must involve at least four nights away within a 12 month period, during which the same activity is pursued.

Who they can do it with

This section offers a high degree of flexibility but it must be done with an organised group, registered charity or Approved Activity Provider.

They must join a residential activity individually and not as part of an existing group of friends. It is acceptable to know a few of the others taking part, but the vast majority should not be people already known to the participant. This is because developing the social skills to establish new friendships and working relationships is an essential part of this section. School or youth group trips are therefore not acceptable.

Participants generally select a project or activity that will see them stay at an activity centre, with a charity, at a youth hostel or camp, but it could be completely different, for example on a tall ship, boat or barge. Staying with friends or relatives is not acceptable.

There are no age restrictions on the people they can do their residential activity with. For example, conservation projects can attract volunteers of all ages from all over the UK, and your participant may be the only one under 25 or doing their DofE.

As their DofE Leader, you and their chosen activity provider should agree in advance that the opportunity meets the section requirements. If your participant is under 18, you need to ensure that safeguarding principles are paramount.

The activity should provide opportunities for broadening interests and experiences. It is ideal for trying something new, or it can be related to existing interests or activities followed in other sections of a programme. For example, a participant may run an after-school club for children with disabilities for their Volunteering section, and then choose to work on a charity's summer camp for children with disabilities. Alternatively, for their Skills section, they may develop a promotional DVD for their youth club following a residential videography course.

Practice and qualifying expeditions are not acceptable for the Residential section.

Preparation is everything

It's vital that the participant thoroughly researches their chosen activity prior to meeting you to discuss their choice. They will then be able to discuss constructively what personal goals should be set. During the meeting you must also cover:

- What the main purpose of the residential is.
- How it will facilitate their self-improvement.
- Whether the residential meets the requirements and conditions of the DofE.
- Any necessary safety or legal requirements.

- Support or training related to health and safety, skills and awareness.
- The process for evaluation and assessment.
- How progress is to be recorded and the format of the final review.

Once you are satisfied that the activity and choice of Assessor meets all requirements, you must gain your OA's approval. With this in place, the participant must tell the relevant organisation that they would like their time with them to count towards their DofE programme.

The Assessor must maintain regular contact with the young person and be fully aware of what their sectional objectives are.

The Handbook for *DofE* Leaders

The Assessor should be briefed about the requirements and aims of the Residential section and be given a copy of the guide to the Residential section leaflet.

Training to make a difference

Initial training may be required so that young people are safe to take part.

Activity, the residential

On arrival at the activity/venue, the participant should remind the course leader that the project will form part of their Gold DofE programme. Meetings should be arranged with the Assessor at the beginning, during and end of the activity to review progress and discuss issues relating to the experience.

Assessment, completing the section

The Assessor must remain in regular contact with the participant throughout their residential activity. Once complete, the participant must discuss their experiences with their Assessor and then they should both enter their comments in the participant's *Record Book*.

Participants should also record:
- How they developed and their progress towards achieving their goals.
- The difficulties they faced and how they overcame them.

Participants will be assessed on:
- Personal standards
- Relationships with others
- Responsibility
- Initiative
- Development of skills
- Knowledge and general progress.

Participants should also have the opportunity to review the quality of experience with their Assessor and enter it in their *Record Book*, which will then be completed by the Assessor. If you are not the Assessor then organise a meeting with the participant to review and discuss their experiences when they return.

*Guidance notes are available to download at **www.DofE.org/residential***

Residential section ideas

For this section, participants need to identify an activity that they want to learn, or improve at, from any of the categories below, that is being done away from home. They then need to set themselves objectives and create their programme to meet them. Listed in each category are examples of programmes that participants could do.

Service to others

Examples:

- Assisting at a summer camp for Brownies.
- Helping out on a pilgrimage to Sri Lanka.
- Aiding deafblind young people and adults to enjoy a holiday.
- Rebuilding a school roof in Lesotho.
- Being an assistant to support an eco-friendly waste project at an outdoor education centre.

Environment and conservation

Examples:

- Attending a conference on climate change as a youth representative for their local authority.
- Studying coral bleaching in Australia.
- Joining a tree planting project in County Antrim with the Woodland Trust.
- Monitoring the bat population in the New Forest.
- Helping the preservation team of a narrow gauge railway in mid Wales.

Learning

Examples:

- Undertaking a cookery course in France.
- Doing a photography course run by a university and exhibiting their work.

The Handbook for *DofE* Leaders

- Learning to snowboard on an intensive course in Scotland.
- Improving their Spanish language skills on a course in Madrid.
- Learning to write and produce music and putting on a show for locals.

Activity based
Examples:
- Taking part in a week-long discovery of stage combat in Wales.
- Joining an ACF activity week with members of different detachments.
- Stewarding at a music festival.
- Taking part in a multi-faith residential, studying different religions and how they interact with each other.
- Joining an historical re-enactment of the Battle of Bosworth.

"It was a definite confidence booster – it helps with your people skills and develops your independence. Doing my DofE has helped me to interact and connect with a huge mix of people of all ages."
Prashan, DofE participant

Chapter 5

Completion, recognition and progression

In this chapter you'll find tips and suggestions to help participants complete their programmes and how to reignite their interest if they're flagging. You can also read about how you can celebrate their achievements and what participants can do after achieving their Gold Award.

5.1   Helping participants to complete their DofE 90

5.2   Sectional certificates 94

5.3   Achieving an Award 94

5.4   Progression 95

5.5   Certificates, badges & Award presentations.....95

5.6   Lost Record Books, certificates & badges 96

5.7   Life after Gold 96

Helping participants complete their DofE

When young people start their DofE programme they do so with an expectation that they will complete it and achieve an Award. In fact, it's important to make it clear to them that the expectation is that because they've started, they'll finish.

Whilst we accept that a small number of participants will not see their programme through to the end, it is important that as many as possible do complete it. It is your responsibility as their DofE Leader to help them achieve this. Below you'll find a list of potential reasons why a participant's attendance may waiver, along with tips on how to address each situation.

Low motivation

Participants can lose heart or feel less energised about achieving their Award as time progresses. To counteract this or even nip it in the bud, regularly talk with them. Find out how they feel, any problems they may be facing and how they could be solved. Celebrate every achievement when you meet them, through sectional presentations, progress charts, information on noticeboards and high profile Award presentations.

Access to activities

Activities are key to all programmes. A young person's interest may decline if they can't do the activities they want or have problems getting to them. Take time at the beginning to help them choose.

By taking the time to talk to participants at the beginning you can manage their expectations about what is available. Talk to them about their interests and help them to choose activities that they're genuinely interested in and will be motivated to do.

One way of re-igniting a participant's interest is by organising group activities which encourage a team spirit e.g. fundraising in the Volunteering section. It's also worth trying taster sessions so that they can get a feel for activities they might not normally have considered.

Wrong choice of activity

To avoid this situation arising, make sure you are aware of all the programme guidelines, are up-to-date with all developments within the DofE and of course the manner in which activities are organised. You can do this by visiting our website, reading our magazine for Leaders and e-newsletter, plus any regional newsletters. It's also worth staying in regular contact with your centre's Co-ordinator, your OA and other Leaders in your region. Remember, if you are in doubt about anything, check with your OA.

If a participant feels that they've selected the wrong activity (though it fits the section), don't forget they can change once at each level.

Only interested in the Expedition section

When you talk with young people about their programme, it's important to impress upon them that ALL the sections offer fun, excitement and adventure.

You may also consider using the Expedition section as encouragement – they can only start it when they finish two other sections; this can often give young people an incentive.

Fear of the Expedition section

At the other end of the scale, some young people may be put off by the thought of an expedition. They may be getting pressure from their peers to do it, be unsure about going to places that are outside their comfort zone or simply feel it's going to be far too tough to do. You can help by talking to them and reassuring them. Remind them that by planning their own route and deciding

how they want to travel, they'll be in control and they can ensure that what they're doing is achievable. Talk them through the training they'll be doing and explain how this will prepare them for their expedition. Using EX^2 can be a fun and easy way to do expedition training.

If it's a fear of the unknown, make sure you show photos of the area and get them to have a look online. You can also arrange a presentation from some older groups who may have experienced the same fears but still completed their expedition.

Not doing or finishing the qualifying expedition

If participants miss their qualifying expedition or cannot complete it for any reason, you can help them to find an alternative. If you are not planning another expedition there are always places available with other groups.

Talk to your DofE Co-ordinator or DofE Manager to find out what is available or check out the opportunities pages on our website.

Lack of kit/equipment

If participants have difficulty getting hold of kit or equipment, check with your centre's Co-ordinator or OA to see if they can help. Sponsorship from local businesses or support from grant awarding bodies may also be a route worth investigating.

Exams

Given the age of participants it's quite likely that their activities will become disrupted by exams. Obviously you cannot expect their programme to take precedence over these, but during this time you can support them from a distance. Keep in contact via phone, emails, newsletters and blogs. Make yourself available to them so that they know they can achieve their Award after their exams.

Too many other things on the go

From Saturday jobs and other clubs, to parties and peer pressure to do other things, many young people find it difficult to fit everything in. With regular mentoring and chats you should be on top of what your participants are doing. Keep a close eye on attendance levels and if things start to drop, chat with them to find out why.

If they are doing too much, it's worthwhile helping them to plan and reprioritise their activities so that they can continue with their programme or see if they can use something they're doing as part of their programme.

Changes in parental circumstances

These can have an emotional and practical impact on a participant's life. If there is upheaval in their family life, attendance at group meetings may wane and they may find it more difficult to get to and from their activities. By keeping in close regular contact with the young person you'll know about potential problems early on.

You can reassure them and ensure that they are aware that they can always return to their programme at any time if they feel unable to continue for the moment. For some, attendance may prove a good distraction. If they do choose to reduce attendance keep in touch via phone (if appropriate), email and newsletters.

Overprotective parents/ guardians/carers

Of course it's only right that a parent or guardian should worry about the safety and well-being of their child. When you organise a recruitment event take time to talk with them about their concerns. Get parents, carers or guardians of current participants to attend and talk

The Handbook for DofE Leaders

about their experiences too. You can also allay concerns and enthuse them about their child's activities during sectional presentations; so take time to talk to the parents, guardians and carers in attendance.

Family holidays, illness and injuries

Always stay in close contact with your participants. Make sure they know that you are ready to help them kick-start activities on their return. If they take time out due to holidays, illness or injury get in touch when they return or recover. Sometimes all it takes is a gentle nudge to get young people back on track.

Lack of transport

If young people are struggling to get to/from their activities, there are ways you can help:
- Talk to them about changing an activity to one that is more easily reached. Many might not be aware they can do this.
- Help them research local public transport options.
- See if any of your other volunteers or older participants could help with transport.
- Other parents within your group may be able to help if young people are doing activities in a similar area – you can facilitate this.

Finances

There are plenty of grant awarding bodies that participants could get in touch with to support them in their adventures, equally local businesses and local authorities can assist too. Make sure participants who are experiencing financial problems are aware of these potential solutions.

Religion/culture

The Duke of Edinburgh's Award is respectful of all cultures and religions. Programmes can be conducted to accommodate all manner of requirements including all-girl groups and religious festivals. As participants design their own programmes they can be developed to accommodate their unique needs. It's important to point this out when recruiting. Ask parents of participants who might relate to the people you are speaking with to talk about their experiences.

Lost Record Books

If a participant loses their *Record Book*, your OA can replace it and endorse any previous entries. There may be a charge for this.

Unsigned Record Books

Many young people complete all their activities and simply forget to get them signed off and sent to your Operating Authority. Make sure they are up-to-date and that you send their books off promptly.

Change/lack of Leader

If you are unable to continue as the DofE Leader for your group, make sure you give your DofE Co-ordinator and/or DofE Manager as much notice as possible, so they can recruit a new Leader. Give them as much help and support as you can to find one and do a handover/training session with the new Leader.

Moving

If a young person is moving out of your area, give them details of their nearest Operating Authority. Stay in touch to encourage them to find a new group and complete their programme.

Many Operating Authorities offer further support to help you raise completion levels.

Sectional certificates

These are available in each section of the Bronze, Silver and Gold levels. They can be issued at your discretion, with the approval of your Operating Authority.

These certificates provide participants with tangible recognition of their progress through each section of their programme. It's also a great way to recognise the achievements of a young person who's unable to complete all sections of their programme.

Achieving an Award

Completing a programme and achieving their Award gives a participant unique experiences and helps develop the skills and attitudes they need to succeed in life. From start to finish, it's one huge adventure that will stay with them forever.

The great thing is that, as a DofE Leader, you'll play a key role in helping young people achieve an Award. You'll be encouraging, supporting and advising them every step of the way; it's a huge but truly fulfilling responsibility.

To gain an Award, the *Record Book* must be authorised by your Operating Authority. For Gold Awards, these must also be approved by the relevant DofE Regional/Country Office.

Please see chapter three, page 33, for more details.

Progression

Once one Award has been achieved and celebrated, your key role as a DofE Leader is to encourage participants to progress to the next level. Return their *Record Book* and talk to them about moving up a level.

Each step up demands more commitment, which is great news for young people who love a challenge. However, it's equally important that you don't leave them feeling overwhelmed at this thought. So allay any concerns or work out how to overcome any issues or difficulties your participant faced during the level they've just finished, to ensure their DofE experience can be continually improved.

It's also worth reminding your participants that they can choose completely different activities for the next level, or choose to keep getting better at the ones they've just been doing – whatever interests them most!

Certificates, badges and Award presentations

Bronze and Silver Award holders receive a certificate and a badge. Gold Award holders receive a certificate and can choose either a badge or a brooch. Images of these can be found at www.DofE.org/gold

Your OA is in charge of deciding how to present Bronze and Silver Awards and many will organise local presentations. If you would also like to arrange one just for your group and/ or centre that's absolutely fine, but let your OA know about your arrangements first. Remember, you must wait until the Awards have been authorised and granted by your OA before organising the presentation.

Gold Award holders are invited to a national presentation at one of the Royal Palaces in the presence of either HRH The Duke of Edinburgh or HRH The Earl of Wessex. These are held throughout the year in England, Scotland and Northern Ireland. The date of their Gold Presentation may be some time after the participant's Award is confirmed but they'll receive an invitation as soon as possible.

For details of Gold Award Presentations please see www.DofE.org/gap

Lost Record Books, certificates and badges

If a participant loses their *Record Book*, the OA can replace it and endorse any previous entries. Participants can also apply to the OA for replacements of any lost Bronze of Silver certificates and badges. There may be a charge for this.

The appropriate DofE Regional/Country Office will deal with any Gold Award badge or certificate replacements, for which there is a small charge. In such cases participants will have to provide evidence that they hold a Gold Award.

Life after Gold

For many people, achieving Gold is just the beginning of their DofE journey. The intensely challenging Gold Award experience is addictive. Continuing their DofE life as a volunteer is the way for our Gold achievers to stay involved and give something back.

Award holders who've recently achieved their Gold Duke of Edinburgh's Award make excellent volunteer DofE Leaders. Some may already have leadership experience, having been DofE Leaders with Bronze & Silver groups for their Volunteering section.

They can also make very inspirational Leaders for participants. This is because participants often relate better to an individual closer to their age who can deal with them on their terms and in their language! Gold Award holders are great role models and give young people something to aspire to.

"The most important attribute I got from doing the DofE was gaining confidence and learning about my strengths. I have been a volunteer Leader for about five years, which has really developed my confidence and I will continue to develop the DofE wherever I am. I feel the DofE has given me so much and I would like to give something back!"
Louise, Gold Award holder

Many young people will automatically be thinking about volunteering and may approach you for help and advice on how to get involved. Others may not have thought about it. You should give them encouragement and let them know that it's possible to become a volunteer Leader and that they would be welcomed as part of your team, especially if you've noticed their potential.

"The young people at my DofE centre are always talking about the importance of recycling. When a group of them achieved their Gold Awards recently, I suggested they 'recycle themselves'. They are now really enjoying helping the next generation of participants through their programmes."
Ian Jones, DofE Leader

So, once you've got their attention, what can you do?

- Run an 'open evening' and leadership taster sessions.
- Give them meaningful, specific roles.
- Use them as ambassadors to go out to speak to potential participants.
- Provide them with training opportunities. Training courses may be provided by you, your centre or your OA.
- Point them to training opportunities at **www.DofE.org/training**
- If they're moving away, help them get in contact with their local OA in their new area. Encourage them to keep in touch.

It is important that new Leaders understand their role and responsibilities, particularly if they have recently been a participant in the same group.
All Leaders are expected to follow the DofE's Code of Behaviour *(see page 108)* and ensure that their relationships with participants are appropriate.

"The DofE has given me the opportunity to give young students with various disabilities the chance to experience and take part in many physically challenging activities. The DofE can be adapted to fit anyone's needs. It has a positive effect on their confidence, teamworking abilities and self-esteem."
Lesley Hedley, DofE Leader

Chapter 6

Other important information and sources of support

This chapter provides you with information about support, training, our partners, our international network and guidance on DofE policies.

6.1	Empowering young people	100
6.2	Support from your Operating Authority	100
6.3	Support from the DofE Charity	102
6.4	Expedition Areas and Co-ordinators	104
6.5	Complaints, feedback and enquiries	104
6.6	National information desk	104
6.7	The International Award Association	105
6.8	Links with other programmes	105
6.9	Approved Activity Providers	105
6.10	Commercial partners	106
6.11	DofE policies	106

Empowering young people

We never forget that young people are at the heart of everything we do.

The DofE encourages Operating Authorities, Co-ordinators and Leaders to involve participants individually, within their peer groups or through forums, in considering how best to use DofE programmes to address:

- The issues that affect their lives.
- How the DofE programme is delivered to help meet those needs.
- How resources are allocated to support that process.

"It's important for programmes such as the DofE to help young people develop. It's very important for Asian young people to take part in the DofE as the social skills gained mean that it's easier to fit into society. It allows people of all backgrounds and races to take part in things that they would otherwise not have the opportunity to do."
Sumiya, Gold Award holder

Support from your Operating Authority

Your Operating Authority is always your main source of support. They will authorise your appointment and support you during the set up of your group.

OAs will clarify the range of services and support they provide through their induction training. This includes the responsibilities outlined in their Operating Authority Licence, but in general you can expect the following:

Ongoing support

Your OA will keep you informed about developments within your area and any programme opportunities. They can let you know how to get hold of any specialist equipment that your participants might need and assist you in organising Award presentations.

As you can imagine, leading a DofE group and/or centre requires administration, so your OA can provide you with a system to help keep things running smoothly. They will also provide you with training, promotional and support material, along with *Record Book Packs*.

Many Operating Authorities offer imaginative ways of support to help participants complete their Awards, for example:

- A weekly surgery for anyone who needs advice and guidance
- Support from a Development Worker when you have a new group
- Extra advice and information sheets
- Certificates of thanks for centres that have high completion rates.

Check with your OA to see what they will do to help you.

Training for success

The success of our programmes relies on the effectiveness of people like you – DofE Leaders who run our programmes. It's your competence and confidence that provides inspirational, high quality experiences for the thousands of young people who aim for an Award.

Your training is an integral part of this support as it enhances the experiences of all participants. This is why we believe everyone should receive quality training according to their needs at local, regional and national levels. In turn this will:

- Achieve consistency in the delivery of programmes to young people
- Promote & share good practice
- Support organisations and individuals in the delivery and development of the DofE programmes
- Keep individuals up to date with new methods of delivery, changes to any criteria and to the DofE Charity itself.

Your OA is responsible for providing suitable learning opportunities for you and your volunteers. This will include an induction as well as regular, appropriate training, support and recognition whilst involved with the DofE.

You may also have access to a range of non-DofE-specific training opportunities through your Operating Authority including, for example, safeguarding and child protection, technical skills training and diversity.

Some of this training can lead to qualifications in youth work and outdoor activities. It may involve meetings, courses, conferences, online and distance learning provided by your OA or DofE Regional/Country Office. Accreditation for Expedition Assessors is also available through the DofE's Expedition Assessor Accreditation Scheme.

You'll find details of the training opportunities available from OAs and DofE Regional/Country Offices at **www.DofE.org/training**

Remember, your Operating Authority is there to help you. So if you do have any questions or need assistance, just get in touch.

Support from the DofE Charity

Website

We provide a wide range of useful resources to help run your DofE group and to promote your activities. For information on everything including new training opportunities, fundraising and the latest expedition advice, make **www.DofE.org** your first stop.

*You'll also find plenty of free downloadable guidance notes on the site at **www.DofE.org/sections** For answers to some of the most common questions we get asked, please visit **www.DofE.org/faq***

Communications

Don't forget to sign up for a free subscription copy of our magazine for DofE Leaders, which is published three times per year at the start of each academic term.

You can also choose to receive our monthly e-newsletter, which delivers the most up to date and relevant information straight to your inbox.

Sign up for both at **www.DofE.org/leaders**

The DofE Modular Training Framework

We created the DofE's Modular Training Framework to give Leaders access to a wide range of flexible, relevant and high quality training opportunities. This guides our trainers and helps volunteers to understand what is available and what skills they can expect to gain.

The framework also means that any training you do is transferable if you move groups – so be sure to ask your OA if they use it.

You can find details of the Modular Training Framework at **www.DofE.org/training**

Current modules include:
- Information/Induction
- Introduction to the DofE
- Managing a DofE group
- Group work skills
- Practical DofE leadership
- Administration
- Expedition Supervisor
- Expedition Assessor Accreditation
- Train the trainer.

e-induction

We have developed an online e-induction programme for any potential or existing DofE Leader. This is free to use and can be accessed at **www.DofE.org/training** – it's the ideal training resource for any new volunteers and as a refresher for anyone who's been a DofE Leader. It will help them understand essential information about the DofE and may be used by some OAs as a pre-requisite for other courses they are running.

Getting your activities noticed

Naturally, you'll need the right resources to promote your group and activities. So for posters and leaflets – available at nominal cost – email our trading arm, ASL on asl@DofE.org or have a look at what's available at **www.DofE.org/shop** Your OA or centre may also provide some material to help you.

All licensed Operating Authorities, approved centres and groups can use the DofE logo – available at **www.DofE.org/logo** along with guidelines on how it should be used.

DofE groups and centres are instrumental in generating local publicity and attracting new entrants and volunteers. Publicity for the DofE can be achieved by:
- Celebrating young people's achievements in your local communities at presentation events and through the local media.
- Publicising information on when your group meets.
- Promoting the activities and successes of your group/centre.
- Engaging the active support of local sponsors and key community figures.

You can find sample press releases and other hints and tips at **www.DofE.org/press**

Expedition Areas and Co-ordinators

Taking part in our wild country expeditions can provide your participants and you with some of the most exhilarating and exciting DofE experiences and memories. But, this will only happen if it's well planned and prepared.

Our expedition networks provide local advice and guidance to help with your preparation.

For a list of Expedition Areas and Co-ordinators visit **www.DofE.org/expedition**

Please see chapter four for details on procedures for communicating with Expedition Areas & Co-ordinators.

Complaints, feedback and enquiries

We define a complaint as when a person wishes to formally register their dissatisfaction with the information or service provided by The Duke of Edinburgh's Award, or the manner in which they were treated.

Most complaints, feedback or enquiries can be dealt with locally by you, the DofE Leader, your DofE Co-ordinator or a DofE Manager at your Operating Authority. Where this is not possible a procedure is set out on our complaints, feedback and enquiries system, which can be read at **www.DofE.org**

If you receive a complaint, please deal with it promptly. Members of the public are unlikely to be able to distinguish between the levels of responsibility within the DofE. If you cannot deal with it, please contact your Operating Authority, who, if necessary, will refer it to their DofE Regional/Country Office.

If it is a child protection issue, The Duke of Edinburgh's Award and Operating Authority Child Protection policy and procedures take precedence, and should be implemented immediately.

National information desk

Our website is bursting with information on all aspects of the DofE. If you need further guidance, please email info@DofE.org or call 01753 727400. Lines are open 09.00-17.00 Monday to Friday except bank holidays.

The International Award Association

This is the governing body for all countries that offer DofE programmes, including the United Kingdom.

DofE programmes now operate in over 120 countries under a variety of titles including, for example, The International Award for Young People, The President's Award, and The National Youth Achievement Award. Whilst the title may vary, the underlying philosophy and basic principles of operation are the same.

Further information can be obtained from:

The International Award Association
Award House
7-11 St Matthew Street
LONDON SW1P 2JT
Tel: 020 7222 4242
Fax: 020 7222 4141
sect@intaward.org
www.intaward.org

Links with other programmes

Participants can use experiences gained with other organisations as part of their programme. This can include, for example, youth clubs, uniformed organisations, higher and further education establishments, businesses and Young Offender Institutes. Activities followed through these partner organisations may count towards their DofE programme, as long as they satisfy the relevant conditions and requirements.

Approved Activity Providers

The Duke of Edinburgh's Award licenses external organisations that provide opportunities which have been proven to meet our conditions and can count towards the achievement of an Award. We call these partners Approved Activity Providers (AAPs). They can be commercial organisations or charities and are usually able to provide a section in its entirety, including accredited assessment and the signing of *Record Books*. As a DofE Leader, you can confidently recommend AAPs to your participants.

It's worth remembering that your OA has the final say on the suitability of AAP programmes in terms of health and safety requirements. So always double check with your OA that the programme is appropriate before using them.

*You'll find a list of current Approved Activity Providers at **www.DofE.org/aap** together with details of how organisations can apply for this status.*

Commercial partners

If a company produces, distributes or retails high quality products that participants could use to help achieve their Award, they can become a DofE licensed commercial partner. In return, we:

- Provide them with a DofE partner logo, which can be used to promote their association with us.
- Allow them to promote their products to OAs, DofE centres/groups and participants.

Endorsed products must meet our quality standards and be suitable for our participants and volunteers.

"Working with participants with special needs is really rewarding. It's great that they are able to participate with their able-bodied friends as equals. I didn't know whether I'd be able to cope but when you see what these young people do and temper that with their ability, or lack of, it's rewarding to see how they progress."
Barry Sinclair, DofE Leader

DofE policies

You must ensure that you and your group abide by the following DofE policies.

Equal opportunities

Never forget that DofE programmes are about inclusion not exclusion. They can be designed to meet the needs of any young person, whatever their ability.

There is no room for discrimination within the DofE. And by that we mean treating a person less or more favourably than another on the grounds of age, race, colour, ethnic origin, nationality, gender, marital status, sexual orientation, disability, health, creed, religious beliefs, class, financial status or caring responsibilities.

Furthermore, we do not discriminate on the grounds of criminal convictions or political beliefs that do not conflict with the aims, principles and policies of the DofE.

Your OA will have its own Equal Opportunities Policy that you must follow too.

If you ever have to ask a participant to leave the group you must inform them that they will remain registered with The Duke of Edinburgh's Award until their 25th birthday. You may be able to help them find a new way to complete their programme. If you need any assistance, your OA or DofE Regional/Country Office will be able to help.

Safeguarding and Child Protection

It is the policy of The Duke of Edinburgh's Award to safeguard the welfare of all young people and others involved in DofE activities by protecting them from physical, sexual and emotional harm.

The Duke of Edinburgh's Award accepts and promotes that in all matters concerning child protection, the welfare and protection of the young person is the paramount consideration.

Safeguarding is about planning and organising activities to prevent potential harm or damage to young people. Child protection is concerned with protecting and/or removing a young person from physical, sexual, emotional abuse or neglect.

The DofE and your Operating Authority have Safeguarding and Child Protection policies and procedures in place. You must ensure that you and any other adults working with you on the DofE are aware of and abide by these.

In particular you must know and understand the steps they should take if they become aware of, suspect or receive allegations of abuse, harassment or bullying.

"I was more than happy to deal with the bit of paperwork to be CRB checked, because it gives parents more peace of mind that their child is in a safer environment."
Sarah Hadley, DofE Leader

Code of Behaviour for DofE Leaders and volunteers

All Leaders and volunteers involved with The Duke of Edinburgh's Award should follow the Code of Behaviour below. You should make sure that everyone in your team is familiar with it. They must also understand your OA's Safeguarding policy and procedures, in particular the steps they should take if they become aware of, suspect or receive allegations of abuse, harassment or bullying.

All Leaders and volunteers involved with The Duke of Edinburgh's Award must:
- Treat everyone with respect
- Act as a good role model of appropriate behaviour.

You must:
- Ensure at least one other person is present when working with a participant or at least be within sight or hearing of others.
- Provide separate sleeping accommodation for DofE Leaders and participants during expeditions and residential activities.

- Remember that actions, remarks and gestures can be misinterpreted, no matter how well intentioned.
- Provide access for participants to talk through any concerns they may have.
- Encourage participants to feel comfortable and care enough to point out attitudes or behaviour they do not like.
- Recognise that caution is required, particularly in sensitive moments.
- Not permit abusive youth peer activities (e.g. initiation ceremonies, ridiculing, bullying, harassment etc.).
- Not have any inappropriate physical or verbal contact with others.
- Not jump to conclusions about others.
- Not react to inappropriate attention seeking behaviour such as tantrums or crushes.
- Not exaggerate or trivialise harassment or child abuse issues.
- Not show any favouritism.

You can download copies of our Code of Behaviour at **www.DofE.org/leaders**

Bullying and harassment

It is the DofE's policy that whilst involved in the programme all young people, Leaders and volunteers are entitled to an environment free from bullying and harassment. You will have support from your OA and the DofE in addressing any type of harassment or related inappropriate behaviour you or they encounter.

Bullying and harassment, in general terms, is unwanted conduct affecting the dignity of an individual or group of individuals. It may be related to age, sex, race, disability, religion, nationality or any personal characteristic of the individual and may be persistent or an isolated incident. The key is that the actions or comments are viewed as demeaning and unacceptable to the recipient. Your Operating Authority is there to help you to deal with any allegations of bullying. If an incident occurs you should seek their support in ensuring that it is dealt with appropriately.

How you can help participants if bullying is occurring

DofE programmes encourage young people to develop their self-confidence and become constructive members of society. Bullying and harassment are unacceptable and taken very seriously. Please feel free to share the following advice on bullying and harassment to your participants and group at large:

- If you feel you are being bullied, whether it is in person, by email, text or online, talk to someone you trust.
- Serious bullying, for example, threats of a physical or sexual nature, should be reported to the police.

- If you can, make a note of the time and date of any incidents.
- Don't forward abusive texts, emails or images to anyone. You could be breaking the law just by forwarding them. If they are about you, keep them as evidence. If they are about someone else, delete them and don't reply to the sender.
- Don't reply to bullying or threatening messages or emails – this could make matters worse. It also lets the bullying people know that they have found a 'live' phone number or email address. They may get bored quite quickly if you ignore them.
- Don't give out your personal details online. If you're in a chatroom, try not to give away any personal information, such as where you live, the school you go to, your email address, etc.
- Don't give out passwords to your mobile phone or email.
- Never bully anyone, or send any bullying or threatening messages. Anything you do, write or send could be reported to an adult.

Remember that sending abusive or threatening messages is against the law.

Care for the environment

The Duke of Edinburgh's Award aims to provide a programme of development for all young people long into the future. Therefore, sustainability of our environment is essential. In light of this we have developed an environmental impact policy, which we all commit to.

The environmental impact policy aims to:
- Promote sustainable use of the outdoor environment.
- Enhance partnerships with the wider community.
- Educate participants about the natural environment and local area.
- Conserve global resources.

Promoting sustainable use of the outdoor environment

- Exercise care and concern for the environment, in line with 'leave no trace' principles.
- Monitor locations used for environmental damage.
- Consider modifying the use of locations to reduce damage.
- Consider assisting with the repair or maintenance of sites, especially if our activities have significantly contributed to that damage.

The Handbook for *DofE* Leaders

Enhancing partnerships with the wider community

- Respect the interests of others, especially those who live, work, manage or carry out their recreation in the environment of our activities.
- Comply with bylaws and access agreements.
- Liaise with landowners, local communities and other organisations over any activities, which may affect them or the land over which they have control, or an interest in.
- Be sensitive to the potential and actual impact of our operation on an area or community.
- Follow the Countryside Code.

Educating participants about the natural environment and local area

- Promote awareness and respect for the natural environment.
- Encourage greater understanding of the natural world and the cultural setting of their surroundings.
- Educate participants as to the appropriate way to enjoy, explore, move or live in the countryside.

Conserving global resources

- Reducing our use of global resources and recycling waste products.
- Using products and materials that support the ethos of the DofE.
- Using materials from sustainable sources and recycled materials.
- Using environmentally efficient equipment.

"I really enjoyed doing my DofE –
it's been an experience I won't forget.
I most enjoyed playing football and
learning woodworking skills."
Josh, DofE participant

Appendices
Other useful information

DofE contact details 114
Glossary of roles and terminology 115
Index 116

DofE contact details

*Contact details for Operating
Authorities can be found at:*
www.DofE.org/contact

www.DofE.org

THE DUKE OF EDINBURGH'S AWARD – HEAD OFFICE
Gulliver House, Madeira Walk,
WINDSOR, Berkshire SL4 1EU
Tel: 01753 727400 Fax: 01753 810666
Email: info@DofE.org

NATIONAL FUNDRAISING TEAM
Award House, 7-11 St Matthew Street,
LONDON SW1P 2JT
Tel: 020 7222 4111 Fax: 020 7222 4112
Email: support@DofE.org

SCOTLAND
Thain House, 226 Queensferry Road,
EDINBURGH EH4 2BP
Tel: 0131 343 0920 Fax: 0131 332 9920
Email: scotland@DofE.org

NORTHERN IRELAND
28 Wellington Park, BELFAST BT9 6DL
Tel: 02890 509550 Fax: 02890 509555
Email: nireland@DofE.org

WALES
Oak House, 12 The Bulwark,
BRECON, Powys LD3 7AD
Tel: 01874 623086 Fax: 01874 611967
Email: wales@DofE.org

MIDLANDS
89-91 Hatchett Street, Newtown,
BIRMINGHAM B19 3NY
Tel: 0121 359 5900 Fax: 0121 359 2933
Email: midlands@DofE.org

SOUTH EAST
South East Regional Office, Gulliver House,
Madeira Walk, WINDSOR, Berkshire SL4 1EU
Tel: 01753 727450 Fax: 01753 810666
Email: southeast@DofE.org

SOUTH WEST
Court Gatehouse, Corsham Court,
CORSHAM, Wiltshire SN13 0BZ
Tel: 01249 701000 Fax: 01249 701050
Email: southwest@DofE.org

NORTH EAST
Maritime Chambers, 1 Howard Street,
NORTH SHIELDS, Tyne & Wear NE30 1LZ
Tel: 0191 270 3000 Fax: 0191 270 3007
Email: northeast@DofE.org

YORKSHIRE & HUMBER
The Yorkshire Waterways Museum,
Dutch River Side, GOOLE,
East Yorkshire DN14 5TB
Tel: 01405 780580 Fax: 01405 721484
Email: yorksandhumber@DofE.org

NORTH WEST
2nd Floor, 20 Mathew Street,
LIVERPOOL L2 6RE
Tel: 0151 231 6220 Fax: 0151 236 6316
Email: northwest@DofE.org

EAST
The Radcliffe School, Aylesbury Street West,
Wolverton, MILTON KEYNES MK12 5BT
Tel: 01908 576322 Fax: 01908 315929
Email: east@DofE.org

LONDON
Award House, 7-11 St Matthew Street,
LONDON SW1P 2JT
Tel: 020 7227 9820 Fax: 020 7222 4112
Email: london@DofE.org

THE AWARD SCHEME LTD (ASL)
www.DofE.org/shop
The Award Scheme Ltd, Unit 18/19
Stewartfield Industrial Estate (off
Newhaven Road), EDINBURGH EH6 5RQ
Tel: 0131 553 5280 Fax: 0131 553 5776
Email: asl@DofE.org

INTERNATIONAL
www.intaward.org
The International Award Association,
Award House, 7-11 St Matthew Street,
LONDON SW1P 2JT
Tel: 0207 222 4242 Fax: 0207 222 4141
Email: sect@intaward.org

Glossary of roles and DofE terminology

Assessor

An adult who checks on a young person's progress and agrees the completion of a section of their programme. They will sign a participant's *Record Book* to confirm this.

In the Expedition section, qualifying expeditions must be assessed by a competent adult who is approved by the Operating Authority and accredited by The Duke of Edinburgh's Award.

DofE centre

A location where the DofE is run, for example, a school, youth centre, Young Offender Institute. There may be one or more groups at a centre.

DofE Co-ordinator

The person who sets up and manages the DofE in a centre. They support the Leaders and oversee the groups.

DofE group

A group of young people who are working together on their DofE programme together, with one DofE Leader.

DofE Leader

The adult responsible for a DofE group. They lead, guide and encourage young people, agree their programme choices and sign off *Record Books*.

DofE Manager

The person in an Operating Authority who is responsible for the day-to-day delivery of the DofE. There will often be other assistants and staff involved.

Operating Authority (OA)

The Operating Authority holds the licence to manage the delivery of DofE programmes and authorise Awards, for example, a local authority, voluntary organisation or independent school.

Participant

Any young person doing a DofE programme.

Supervisor

A person with a good understanding of a participant's chosen activities. They will help set goals and regularly meet with the young person to check on their progress, address any potential issues and adjust goals.

A Supervisor is essential for the Expedition section as they are responsible for supervising and supporting a team of participants to ensure their safety and well-being whilst they are doing their expedition.

Volunteer/helper

Any adult who helps a DofE Leader run a group. They may give general support, i.e. administration, help run one section or give specific training.

A more detailed glossary is available on **www.DofE.org**

Index

A

Activities prior to entry 30
Addresses (DofE Offices) 114
Affordability..17
Age 24-27
ASL 103, 114
Assessment...32
Assessors........................... 18, 76, 115
Assessor Accreditation 76
Authorisation of Awards............................33
Award Presentations.............................95

B

Badges...95
Benefits 4
Breaks...31
Bullying and harassment........................109

C

Centre 5, 115
Certificates 95
Challenging programmes.........................30
Changing activities..................................33
Charity; the DofE 5, 102
Child protection and
    safeguarding...........................10, 107
Choices 37
Choosing activities 29
Code of Behaviour..............................108
Commercial partners 106
Complaints, feedback & enquiries..........104
Completion......................................90-94
Co-ordinators 5, 115

E

e-induction 103
Empowering young people 100
Environmental impact 110-111
Equal opportunities............................3, 106
EX² 65
Expedition Areas & Co-ordinators..........104
Expedition section 63-79
    20 conditions............................70-71
    Accommodation 68

Adventurous projects 73
Aim 63
Approved Activity Providers 77
Assessors 76, 115
Assessor accreditation.........................76
Benefits 63
Debrief..69
Environments 67
Equipment 68
Expeditions outside the UK 72
Ideas..78-79
Multiple teams 72
Open expeditions.................................77
Practice expedition(s)...........................66
Preparation 64
Presentation...69
Principles 63
Process 64
Publications & materials 77
Qualifying expedition 66
Safety 74
Supervisors.................................75, 115
Timescales...66
Training 65
Variations 72
Wild country..................................67, 68

F

Finances.................................12, 16, 17, 93

G

Gold Award holders................................96
Group..5, 14, 115
Guiding principles 3

I

Insurance 12
International Award Association 105

L

Leaders 5, 10, 115
    Role & responsibilities 10-13, 36
Levels...23
Lost Record Books, certificates
    and badges 96
Logo...103

M

Magazine 102
Manager, DofE 5, 115
Moving 94

N

National information desk 104

O

Operating Authorities 5, 115
    Role 6
    Support 100-101
Other programmes 105

P

Parents, carers and guardians 15
Participation fees 16
Personal time 28
Physical section 47-53
    Activity 50
    Aim 47
    Assessment 50
    Benefits 47
    Ideas 52-53
    Preparation 49
    Principles 47
    Process 48
    Timescales 49
    Training 50
Policies 106
Presentations 95
Process 31-32
Programmes 2, 22
Progression 33, 95
Publicity 103

R

Record Book 16
Residential section 81-87
    Activity 85
    Aim 81
    Assessment 85
    Benefits 81
    Ideas 86-87
    Preparation 84
    Principles 81
    Process 82

Timescales 83
Training 85
Who with 83

S

Safety 10
Safeguarding and child
    protection 10, 107
Sectional certificates 94
Shop 103, 114
Skills section 55-61
    Activity 58
    Aim 55
    Assessment 58
    Benefits 55
    Ideas 60-61
    Preparation 57
    Principles 55
    Process 56
    Timescales 57
    Training 57
Starting a group 14
Starting a programme 28, 33
Structure 5
Supervisors 19, 75, 115

T

Time 24-27, 37
Training (Leaders and
    volunteers) 101, 102, 103

V

Volunteering section 39-45
    Activity 42
    Aim 39
    Assessment 43
    Benefits 39
    Ideas 44
    Preparation 41
    Principles 39
    Process 40
    Team volunteering 39
    Timescales 41
    Training 41
Volunteers 17, 115

W

Website 102